THE CLASSICS OF WESTERN SPIRITUALITY

THE CLASSICS OF WESTERN SPIRITUALITY
A Library of the Great Spiritual Masters

President and Publisher
Kevin A. Lynch, C.S.P.

EDITORIAL BOARD

Ibn 'Ata' Illah
THE BOOK OF WISDOM

Kwaja Abdullah Ansari
INTIMATE CONVERSATIONS

INTRODUCTION, TRANSLATION AND NOTES
OF
The Book of Wisdom by VICTOR DANNER
AND OF
Intimate Conversations by WHEELER M. THACKSTON

PREFACE
BY
ANNEMARIE SCHIMMEL

PAULIST PRESS
NEW YORK • RAMSEY • TORONTO

Cover Art:
The artist EDWARD F. BARBINI studied painting and advertising art and design at Pratt Institute and The School of Visual Arts before embarking on a career as a designer and Art Director for various New York ad agencies. In 1966 he became a principal of the Barbini, Pesce and Noble Advertising Agency, where he is currently Executive Art Director. Mr. Barbini is a member of the New York Art Directors Club and winner of various advertising awards including the prestigious "Andy" award. Mr. Barbini has exhibited his paintings at various art shows in the New York Metropolitan area. Of his cover painting he says, "The painting, while done in a modern style, embodies the essence of traditional Persian and Islamic art. Through the combined use of simple line and loose watercolor the painting captures the aphoristic nature of the *Book of Wisdom* and the simplicity of *Intimate Conversations*."

Design: Barbini Pesce & Noble, Inc.

Copyright © 1978 by the Missionary Society
of St. Paul the Apostle
in the State of New York

Library of Congress Catalog Card Number: 78-1022

ISBN: 0-8091-2182-4 (Paper)
0-8091-0279-X (Cloth)

Published by Paulist Press
Editorial Office: 1865 Broadway, New York, N.Y.   10023
Business Office: 545 Island Road, Ramsey, N.J.   07446

Printed and bound in the United States of America

CONTENTS

The Editors of this Volume:

VICTOR DANNER, born in Mexico in 1926, raised and educated in America, is Associate Professor of the Arabic Language and Literature at Indiana University. After military service in the Second World War, he earned a B.S. degree in Arabic Studies at Georgetown University and taught for seven years in Morocco, serving also as Administrator of the American Language Program supported by the American Embassy in Rabat. He received his doctorate in Near Eastern Languages and Literatures from Harvard in 1970.

Since 1967, Professor Danner has taught Arabic and Arabic Literature, Islam, Sufism, the Eastern Religions, and Comparative Mysticism in the Departments of Near Eastern Languages and Literatures and Religious Studies at Indiana University. The author of a number of articles on Islamic mysticism for learned journals, his book *Sufi Aphorisms* was published in 1973. That same year he participated in the first International Conference on Traditional Modes of Contemplation and Action in Houston, Texas, which was attended by representatives of the different world faiths.

In the 1976-77 academic year he participated in a world tour with faculty and students from a number of American universities, studying Islam, Hinduism, and Buddhism, under the sponsorship of the International Honors Program. A Sufi specialist, Professor Danner feels that he owes the deepening of his knowledge to first-hand observations of Sufi adherents and their institutions during his stay in Morocco.

WHEELER MCINTOSH THACKSTON, JR., born in Greenville, South Carolina in 1944, is Assistant Professor of Iranian Languages and Literatures in the Department of Near

Eastern Languages at Harvard University. A Persian Language and Literature specialist, he earned his A.B. degree at Princeton University in 1967, and his Ph.D. degree at Harvard in 1974.

Professor Thackston has been the recipient of a number of prestigious fellowships including that of the National Undergraduate Program for Overseas Study in Arabic at the Middle East Centre for Arab Studies in Chemlan, Lebanon, the Woodrow Wilson Graduate Fellowship, the National Defense Education Act Title IV Fellowship, the Harvard Travel Fellowship, and the U.S.-Iran Bicentennial Research Grant.

The author of a growing list of publications and papers in *Persian Studies*, he is also the General Editor of the *Anthology of Contemporary Persian Prose Literature* and the *Anthology of Contemporary Persian Poetry* for the Iranian Studies Series of the Centre Iranien pour le Dialogue des Civilisations, Teheran. He has also served as the Director of the English Institute for Secondary School Teachers at Mashhad University, Mashhad, Iran during the summer of 1971.

ANNEMARIE BRIGITTE SCHIMMEL, born in Erfurt, Germany, in 1922, earned doctorate degrees at both Berlin University and Marburg University. She has held professorships in Islamic Studies at Marburg University, Bonn University, and since 1967, at Harvard University. She is a member of several scholarly societies, among them The Middle East Studies Association, The Association for the Study of Religion, The British Oriental Society, and The German-Iranian Association. A contributor of articles to professional journals, she is also the author of a number of books, including *Mystical Dimensions of Islam*.

Preface

It was a night of despair, a cold October night, 1945, in Germany. We were sitting in a dirty railway station, lucky to have found at least one place where to spend the night after long and uncomfortable travelling. People around me tried to sleep, or talked about the horrors of the war, of imprisonment, of hunger. . . . I took from my coat's pocket a small book that had survived wartime Berlin, deportation, and internment, and had given me unending consolation during those years.

What use has he of his soul who has known You?
What use has he of offspring and family?

Thus said Abdullah-i Ansari in his *Munajat*, which I had found in the Berlin print of 1924 some time during the war. Once more I delved into its depths, scribbled some rhyming translations of its pithy sayings and verses between the lines, and was carried away from the "world" in its ugliest aspects into the realm of peace:

O God,
those who labor for wages are content with You,
but those who know You are indifferent to past and
    future.

For some precious moments I felt the proximity of God whom the mystics have always invoked in hope and fear; who was their beloved and the final goal of their quest. Thirty years later I took the small book to Herat to thank Ansari for the help his work had given me. Indeed, Ansari's *Munajat* can be prayed even today, the artistic quality of the Persian rhyming prose and the inserted quatrains notwithstanding. The reader encounters here the wisdom of a searching and suffering man, who pours out his feelings in the presence of the Lord like little sighs, for the rhythm of these prayers is like breathing in its constant change of contraction and expansion.

This same quality also permeates the *Hikam* and *Munajat* of another Sufi, who lived more than 200 years later and several thousand miles' distance from Ansari's Herat, in Egypt, and who belonged to a different linguistic environment. While Ansari's *Munajat* were and still are the favorite subject for meditation in the Persian-speaking world and were often beautifully written by the master calligraphers of Iran, Ibn 'Ata'il-lah's sayings have played the same role in the Arabic-speaking areas, their fame extending even farther: Turkish commentaries exist as well as collections made in India (such as by 'Ali al-Muttaqi in the 16th century). While Père de Beaureceuil has rediscovered the religious importance of the patron saint of Herat and put his many sided work before us, Père Nwyia has called Ibn 'Ata'illah's *Hikam* "the last Sufi miracle worked on the shores of the Nile."

Both authors belong to strictly lawbound schools of Islam: Ibn 'Ata'illah was a scholar of Malikite law, Ansari a stern Hanbalite (the same legal school to which Ibn 'Ata'illah's adversary, Ibn Tai-miyya, belonged!). Both knew that the *shari'a*, the main road of revealed law, is the necessary foundation for the *tariqa*, the narrow path that branches off from the highway and may lead the wayfarer to the realization of the experience of the Divine already in this life, not only at the Day of Judgment. For the mystic who embarks upon the difficult and hard path has to "die before he dies" so that he can be spiritually resurrected.

It seems important to me that in both Ansari's and Ibn 'Ata'illah's case the lawbound attitude is prevalent; for this is a good antidote against all too many modern interpretations of

Sufism whose representatives see in "Sufism" nothing but a spiritual uplifting; an enjoyable movement of the soul, not fettered by the tradition of any revealed religion; a kind of free thinking; a pretext for indulging in poetry, music, and dance. Such an attitude had been criticized as early as in the 11th century by Ansari's compatriot Hujwiri (with whom he shares the honor of having composed the first Sufi works in the Persian language).

The modern reader who approaches both the Arabic *Hikam* with their *munajat* and the Persian *Munajat* without any deeper knowledge of Sufi history will immediately be captured by the beauty of the language—a language which no translation can reproduce adequately. For the Sufis had developed a special technique of hints and allusions: In every word a whole range of related concepts is concealed, so that the deeper layers of meaning unveil themselves only to the patient reader after repeated meditation. This language had been developed in the 9th and 10th centuries by mystics like Yahya ibn Mu'adh whose prayers became models for all later "intimate conversations" with God. The mature wisdom of Junaid's definitions contributed to their formation as much as did the glowing dialectics of Hallaj's utterances. And the brevity of both *Hikam* and *Munajat* proves the immense self-control of the mystics who were able to condense their deepest feelings and their loftiest experiences in small, gemlike, perfectly polished sayings.

Even, without knowing the linguistic and historical background of these works, the reader feels and is moved by the depth of religious experience. It is an experience whose expressions appeal to us as if they had been written today. The constant tension between the two aspects of the Revealed God (Creator, Sustainer, and Judge)—e.g., his *jamal*, Beauty, Kindness, and Grace, and his *jalal*, Majesty, Justice, and Wrath (formulated as an important category in the history of religions by Rudolf Otto in his book *The Experience of the Holy*)—this tension is palpable in both the *Hikam* and the *Munajat*. How to explain the acts of God who can be apparently cruel and yet is The Merciful? A saying like this:

> Sometimes He gives while depriving you, and sometimes He deprives you in giving

is as much food for thought as the consoling words about prayer:

> When He loosens your tongue with a request,
> then know that He wants to give you something.

In a time when selfishness and desire for wealth seem to prevail among people, is it not useful to read Ibn 'Ata'illah's word about gratitude:

> Whoever is not thankful for graces runs the risk of
> losing them; and whoever is thankful, fetters them
> with their own cords.

Here he elaborates ideas that are expressed in poetry by his older contemporary in Anatolia, the great mystical poet Rumi. Is not gratitude for everything that happens the best way to overcome the difficulties of life? Ibn 'Ata'illah speaks of the importance of the "night of contraction," taking over an idea of Junaid, and lays the foundation for some of the wisest sayings of his follower and commentator, Ibn 'Abbad of Ronda, whose aim was to transform man's whole life into a constant act of rendering grace. Man should learn to see God's hand even in the darkest moments of life, and to thank Him for whatever He sends; for, as the Persian mystics would poetically elaborate this central idea: The Sun at Midnight rises only in the "dark night of the soul," or: The water of life is found in the darkest valley . . . . One has to learn that even enemies are a means to drive man toward God, and that there is nothing in the world which does not conceal some positive value—provided one has eyes to see, and gives his heart and will completely in God's hand. But even obedience may be a veil that hinders man from spiritual progress because it makes him proud and self-conscious; that is why Ansari cries out:

Happy that disobedience that brings me to my knees!

God, often forgotten in the days of joy, can be found more easily in darkness and repentance.

It is often difficult for modern man to enjoy the enthusiastic utterances of Oriental mystics, the stories of complete poverty and exaggerated asceticism, of incredible miracles; for we have become afraid of big words, of pious pretensiousness, and avoid making a show of our religious feelings. For this reason Ibn 'Ata'illah's *Hikam* and Ansari's *Munajat* are likely to appeal to a modern reader more than mystical verses (whose whole charm, in any case, is lost in translation). Born of great spiritual experiences and deep wisdom, these words are still sober, almost austere. Therefore they may be enjoyed even by readers who have no outspoken "mystical" inclinations. They offer a perfect code of life: complete trust in God, deep faith in His grace and awareness of His justice, and an insight into His mysterious working through the contrasting manifestations of this created world. Thus, they slowly lead the reader toward the highest goal, e.g., the realization of man's inner values in the unquestioning fulfillment of "*Islam*", that will say, of giving one's self completely in God's hand and working in conformity with what one experiences as His will. The sighs of Ansari can be repeated by every human being, who will feel that in many a moment he would have liked to express his hope, his despair, his trust in God in similar words.

To return to these two small vademecums of medieval

PREFACE

Sufi literature should prove an enriching experience for those who are in need of a handbook of spiritual life into which to look time and again for guidance in the day of joy, and for hope in the night of despair.

Annemarie Schimmel

Ibn 'Ata'illah

The Book of Wisdom

(Kitab al-Hikam)

Introduction and Translation

by

Victor Danner

Acknowledgements

Many thanks are due to Professor George Makdisi, now of the University of Pennsylvania, for his excellent advice and guidance; to Dr. Martin Lings, formerly of the British Museum, for his help; and to Titus Burckhardt for many suggestions regarding the translation.

We must also indicate our appreciation to the various Arabic manuscript libraries for their kind assistance: the British Museum, Fatih, Tübingen, the Bibliothèque Nationale, and the Escorial.

Foreword

Ibn 'Ata'illah, the author of the *Kitab al-Hikam* [The Book of Aphorisms], was a Sufi sage and saint of 13th-century Egypt. His works loom large on the historical horizon as the earliest written documents of the Sufi order Shadhiliyyah, which was founded shortly before his time and still exists throughout the Muslim world. He was himself a spiritual master of that order and hence is called Shaykh Ibn 'Ata'illah. Among his works, the *Kitab al-Hikam* is particularly noteworthy because of its universal value. It has a timeless quality that turns it into an ever-fresh affirmation of the life of the Spirit in man. As far as we can tell, it was written sometime before the death of his master, Shaykh Abu 'l-'Abbas al-Mursi, in 1288. It has about it the perfume of mystical realization that has endeared it to countless generations of Sufi adherents in the world of Islam and to pious Muslims in general, who have been attracted by its simple, aphoristic nature and its comprehensive coverage of the essentials of the Sufi Path. Written in charming, rhythmical, and yet solemn and dignified Arabic, the work lends itself to memorization in that tongue, and many Muslims, both within and outside of the Sufi tradition, have learned its contents by heart and turned them over in their minds meditatively. Probably the author chose that aphoristic and rhythmical style deliberately as a didactic medium for the diffusion of fundamental Sufi concepts and attitudes over as wide an audience as possible. His work also represents a joyous summation of the spiritual way by one who experienced it himself in all its directness and luminous nature, and who wished to make known to others the path leading to union with the Absolute that Islam calls *Allah*. Its popularity in the mystical and pious circles of the Islamic world down to our days attests to the author's success in embodying within the confines of a small book the essence of the spiritual life in the Islamic religion.

In the pages that follow, the reader will find, first, an introduction that deals in succinct fashion with the life and works of Ibn 'Ata'illah; second, the translation of the *Kitab al-Hikam*, with footnotes for those aphorisms, concepts, and terms that need further clarification; third, a glossary of Sufi technical terms that are fundamental for an understanding of the text; and, fourth, a brief general bibliography of readings for those who want more information or perhaps more doctrinal background on the Sufi Path represented by this author.

Introduction

In seeking to understand the life and works of Shaykh Ibn 'Ata'illah, we must remember that he was part of a living mystical and religious tradition that antedated him by long centuries. He was raised in the matrix of the Islamic faith, and he died therein, having contributed in his own way to the spiritual regeneration of his tradition, not only through his saintly example, but also through his writings. He was a flower of that tradition, so it is best to approach him through his Islamic background rather than subject him to the scrutiny of a non-Islamic viewpoint, which could not provide us with the criteria or norms that would make sense out of his life and works.

The Islamic tradition he was born into was based on the Qur'anic Revelation, on the one hand, and on the Sunnah (Norm) of the Prophet Muhammad, on the other; they were the two foundations of the Islamic religion, and have remained such down to our times. How one looked at those two, however, determined whether one belonged to exoteric or esoteric Islam—the former being that of the majority of Muslims, who were engaged in action, the latter being that of the minority of Muslims, who were engaged in contemplation. Sufism, by its very nature, is esoteric; formalistic and literalistic Islam is exoteric. The great mass of Muslims, then as now, followed the exoteric facet of the Islamic Message and had salvation as their goal, implying the posthumous entry into Paradise. Only a minority of the faithful were in one or another of the Sufi orders, which does not mean that they did not observe the prescriptions of the exoteric Law—they did observe them, but, being mystical, they also observed the discipline of the Path, which has as its goal the salvific love and knowledge of God.

INTRODUCTION

That was the Islam that Shaykh Ibn 'Ata'illah inherited. It had been in existence for almost six and a half centuries by the time he came into the world. Like all other eminent Sufi teachers throughout history, he was raised as a Muslim in exoteric Islam, and he never ceased being one and fulfilling, throughout his life, the prescriptions of the Law of Islam. But, in addition, he was a Sufi esoterist, which means that he possessed a contemplative intelligence that allowed him to see a much deeper dimension to the Islamic Revelation, and even to the world around him, than was the lot of the conventional Muslim. His Sufism cannot be understood without that Islamic faith and that is a point one must never forget in seeking to understand the Sufi Path. There is no such thing as Sufism *and* Islam, for such a concept creates a false dichotomy between mysticism and religion that the authetic Sufi masters, including Shaykh Ibn 'Ata'illah himself, would summarily reject. Yet, there is such a thing as Sufism *in* Islam, and indeed Sufism is considered by its authorities as the most profound nature of the Islamic Revelation.

When we come across the Shaykh at the peak of his career, he is a Sufi master, and therefore a spiritual authority of the Path; but he had already been in his younger years a doctor of the Law, a religious authority in his own right; thus, he combined in his person authority over the two dimensions of the Islamic religion, the esoteric and the exoteric. It must not be thought that the Sufism of his day was simply of one unique brand, no more than it is nowadays; on the contrary, it was represented by numerous Sufi orders, each one having numerous masters and thousands of disciples. His own order was called the Shadhiliyyah and had only recently come into being, its founder, the illustrious Shaykh Abu'l-Hasan ash-Shadhili, having died in Egypt when Ibn 'Ata'illah was around six years of age. In time, he became the third great master of the Shadhiliyyah, an order that has played a most important role in the spiritual life of the Islamic world in the last eight centuries. Today it is one of the most important—if not the most important—of the numerous Sufi orders (such as the Qadiriyyah, the Chishtiyyah, the Suhrawardiyyah, and others) scattered over the face of the Muslim world.

The world view of Ibn 'Ata'illah was a religious one. Everything—theology or philosophy, art or architecture, literature or music, the city or the countryside—was touched, in one way or another, by the Islamic spirit. From the smallest drinking cup to the most impressive Mamluk dwelling or palace, the stamp of Islam was everywhere. That world view is still operative, to a certain extent, in the present-day Muslim world, though it has clearly lost quite a bit of its aesthetic element. But Ibn 'Ata'illah had nothing to invent for himself since everything was provided for him by the all-enveloping tradition. It came to him simply by virtue of the fact that he was a Muslim of Mamluk days in Egypt; the classic structures of his civilization had been laid down centuries before his time. He had only to make the proper gestures and responses and the rest would take care of itself, but he had nothing to fabricate with his own hands. Obviously, such a world had a teleological signification of persuasive force for the intelligent Muslim of good will, and that was what Ibn 'Ata'illah was, his Sufism simply deepening his fine qualities and finally transforming them into spiritual energies.

Sufism as the Path

Much of what is found in the works of Ibn 'Ata'illah, and more particularly in his *Kitab al-Hikam*, represents what could be called the core or essence of Sufism, based on the Qur'an and the Sunnah, as previously mentioned. Sufism, as an independent contemplative Path, detached itself from the juridico-theological schools, such as the Malikite and the Hanbalite, that arose in the 9th century in response to social, political, and religious pressures that the nascent Islamic civilization experienced from within. From then on, Sufism led an independent existence within the Islamic fold, its authorities (the Shaykhs of the Path) being quite distinct from the ordinary exoteric authorities of the Law, even though, from time to time, conflicts and clashes would occur, mostly provoked by the jealousy or envy of the doctors of the Law. Centuries later, Ibn 'Ata'illah would inherit, as part of his Sufism, the institutional life that Sufism had developed from early days. He belonged to one of the four schools of Islamic exoterism, namely, the Malikite; thus, both his Malikism and his Sufism go back to the early days of Islam, his orthodoxy in both domains being irreproachable.

Sufism can be defined as Islamic spirituality, that is to say, it has to do with the life of the Spirit in an immediate sense, and as such it has to do with the *tariqah*, which means generically the spiritual Path, as distinguished from the *shari'ah*, or the sacred Law. When dealing with Sufism, it is best to leave to one side such terms as "mystic" and "mysticism," if only because in the modern Western world such words nowadays often lead to confusion. In the rather loose manner in which they are used, they are inappropriate to describe Ibn 'Ata'illah and his teachings. If everyone in the West understood by mysticism such teachings and practices as found in the Greek Fathers of the Church, the Hesychasts, Meister Eckhart of medieval Catholicism, and Plotinus, then Sufism is indeed mysticism, and the Sufis are mystics; but in the West the most conflicting opinions exist on what constitutes mysticism, due no doubt to the absence of anything resembling the permanent tradition of Islamic Sufism. That being the case, the term "Sufism" is best left intact; so long as it is understood as a body of teachings and methods having the love and knowledge of God as their goal, it cannot be confused with the aberrant forms of mysticism so rampant in modern times in the West.

As previously mentioned, Sufism considers itself to be the very essence of Islam—and even its spiritual heart—and not something extraneous to that religion. Nevertheless, certain Neoplatonist notions intruded themselves into the Sufi formulations from the 9th century onward because the translations from Greek philosophical works into Arabic had affected the mental climate in the Muslim world and introduced a certain analytical process of thinking that was in direct contrast to the more synthetic vision of Revelation that the earlier Muslims had entertained. But the intrusion of Neoplatonist thought into Sufism did not create a radical transformation of the Islamic Path; that thought, after all, while more analytical, merely carried a step further many of the germinal reflections and inspirations of earlier Sufis on the divine Unity (*tawhid*), the macrocosm and the microcosm, and their interrelationships. And, in any case, such Neoplatonist ideas, once Islamicized, were seen by the Sufi sages who used them to be perfectly compatible with their own intuitions of a doctrinal nature.

The term "Sufi" and its cognates were of course of later origin than the Qur'anic Revelation, but this does not mean, in the eyes of the Sufis, that the Path itself is of later invention. As they see things, the Path and the Law (*tariqah* and *shari'ah*) are both of revealed origin, that is to say, of celestial nature, and began with the Prophet himself. It was only later, in the 8th and 9th centuries, when the need for clarification and codification was felt in every single department of the Islamic faith, that the word "Sufi" came into being, precisely at the same time as such epithets as Hanbalite, Malikite, Shafi'ite, and Hanafite came into being to describe the various schools of exoteric Islam. Therefore, Sufi esoterism arose at the very moment that the legalistic exoterism of Islam began to crystallize into schools, institutions, and personalities. The reality of the Path, however, had always been there since the origin of the religion in the days of Muhammad; what had changed was the social, moral, political, cultural, and religious atmosphere of Islam as it spread out to embrace literally millions of human souls and to give rise to its great world civilization. Something had to give in the process, and that something was the previous homogeneity and synthetic Message of the faith: Like a tree gradually growing out of a sapling, the tradition became more complex and ramified; the esoterism and exoterism that had formerly been more intimately wedded in the archaic tradition of Islam now split apart and went their separate ways, but without divorce. Each soon developed in its own fashion, with its own teachers, methods, doctrines, terminology, and perspectives. The doctors of the Law, the 'ulama', wielded tremendous power in the social and political world of Islam, as they did in the religious sphere; they were the religious authorities of Islam, and the great mass of Muslims followed their authority without demur. As for the contemplatives, they rallied around the Sufi Shaykhs of the Path, who very often also had quite an influence on the people at large; the cult of Sufi saints and their shrines all over the Islamic world attests to the popular repercussions that Sufism has always provoked during its long, millenial history.

As was said, the Law of Islam has in view the posthumous salvation of the individual, with all that this implies in the way of the beatific vision of the Divinity in Paradise; while Sufism has in view the love and knowledge of the Divinity here and now, implying a liberation or salvation that is effective immediately, in this very life, and not postponed till the Hereafter. But that love and knowledge of the Real could also be described as a loving knowledge of God or a knowing love of Him, and this is what the Sufis mean by ma'rifah, or "gnosis." That gnosis is not just a knowledge of God, for it cannot be had without the love of the Real; nor is it just a love of God, for it cannot be had without the knowledge of the Real, the Real

(*al-Haqq*) being but another name for God in Islam, one of the
ninety-nine "beautiful Names" of the Divinity, as the Qur'an
describes them. Gnosis is not possible in Sufism without that
mixture of love and knowledge which characterizes the saintly
sage, or the wise saint. Hence, *ma'rifah* is considered the very
summit of the spiritual Path in Sufism; the gnostic is he who
possesses perfect knowledge and love of the divine Absolute
called *Allah*. As a result, one must not confuse Sufism with the
various forms of asceticism and devotionalism that the spiritual
life in Islam can take, since these are only truncated and in any
case fragmentary ways of approaching God, as the aphorisms
of Shaykh Ibn 'Ata'illah themselves lead us to believe; and it
could very well be that one of the original causes behind the
appearance of the term "Sufism" (*tasawwuf* in Arabic) in the 8th
century was precisely the desire of the early masters to set the
total Path of gnosis apart from the lesser ways of asceticism and
devotionalism, which threatened to become ends in themselves.

Gnosis eventually became the preferred term in Sufism to
describe the goal of the Path, although other terms are also
used, likewise implying knowledge of the divine mysteries and
realities. But it should not be confused with any special type of
Gnosticism that existed in the early Christian Church—being
heretical in its teachings as well as heteroclite and syncretistic
in its absorption of non-Christian elements, such Gnosticism
was in stark contrast with the quite legitimate gnosis of the
Greek Fathers and of the later Hesychasts. The *ma'rifah* of
Sufism is not something occultist or bizarre; as understood by
the Sufis, gnosis comes with ever-deepening faith, and not
contrary to it or outside of it. Nor is it possible for anyone
dispossessed of the fear or respect of the Divinity to reach that
gnosis through a kind of backdoor to the Path, for there is
none. Therefore, one should add to the concepts of love and
knowledge that attach themselves to Sufi gnosis the notion of

the reverential fear of God, which breeds a distrust of the world as other-than-God, and prepares the way for the love and knowledge of the Real.

The Life of Shaykh Ibn 'Ata'illah

Ibn 'Ata'illah was born into a prestigious religious dynasty in Alexandria, Egypt, somewhere around the middle of the 13th century. He spent most of his life in that land, and died there in 1309. Under its Mamluk sultans, who had just come to power when Ibn 'Ata'illah entered the world and was growing up, Egypt had become the political and religious center of the eastern part of the Islamic world—once the Caliphate had been destroyed in Baghdad by the Mongols in 1258, the Mamluk sultans were able to recreate the Caliphate in Cairo and declare themselves its ruling representatives. Ibn 'Ata'illah lived during the entire legendary career of Sultan Baybars and the early Mamluk rulers, whose exploits in the political, military, religious, and artistic domains were responsible for giving a renewed vitality to the Islamic faith. They were the ones who had checked the Mongols east of Egypt and destroyed their forces, thus signaling the end of Mongolian expansion westward and the beginning of their political and military decline in the Near East. They were the ones who had suppressed, once and for all, the power of the Isma'ilis (the "Assassins" of the Middle Ages) and thus ended the divisive role of this Shi'ite sect, which at one point wielded impressive military strength through its many fortresses in the eastern world of Islam. They were the ones who finally conquered the last-remaining strongholds of Christianity in the Levant, ending the Crusades and returning to Islam the lands occupied by the Christian rulers and their troops. And, finally, they were the ones who gave the Sunnite world of Egypt and Syria, over which they ruled, a much more homogeneous nature, encouraging also the construction of numerous mosques, religious schools, and Sufi meeting-houses. Shaykh Ibn 'Ata'illah himself taught in one of the religious schools built by the Mamluks, and he became one of the guiding lights of Sufism in the Egypt of his day. It was, thus, during a period that saw a good deal of the past achievements of the Muslims destroyed by the Mongols and that saw, on the ashes of those ruins, a powerful readaptation of the Islamic culture and body politic by the Mamluks of Egypt and Syria that Ibn 'Ata'illah lived and carried out his function as Sufi Shaykh in Cairo, not to mention his role as the first of the early Shadhilite masters to write down the teachings, thereby leaving to posterity the earliest formulations of the Sufi order he belonged to (its first two masters never having written any books at all).

But before going into his life, it is well to situate him within that revitalization of Sufi spirituality that was so evident in the 13th century, a period that played a determining role in laying the foundations, both intellectual and spiritual, for the future centuries of Islam. Since Sufism is seen by its adherents as the heart of Islam, whatever happens to it, happens to the religion as a whole, just as, in the human body, the state of the physical heart affects man's body as a whole. What happened in the 13th century was that a veritable eruption of Sufism took place, and this contrasted markedly with the disruptions and even destructions of entire peoples and cultures in the different provinces of the Levant at the hands of the Mongols: destruction on one side, construction on the other. It is doubtful that Sufism could have been so explosively effective on the social scene if society itself had not been stirred to its depths by the menace of fire and steel represented by the Mongolian invasions. Sufism provided a kind of "second Revelation" for the Islamic tradition as a whole in those days, and it did so via two phenomena of extraordinary importance, both of which would affect Shaykh Ibn 'Ata'illah. The first phenomenon is situated on the intellectual plane of Sufi doctrinal formulations and is represented by the great Ibn al-'Arabi (d. 1240), the Andalucian Sufi sage whose sanctity and literary production justly prove the title of *ash-Shaykh al-Akbar* ("the Most-Great Master") that Sufism has bestowed on him. His doctrine of *wahdat al-wujud*, or "the Oneness of Being," expressed in numberless works — particularly in his *al-Futuhat al-Makkiyyah* [The Meccan Revelations] and the *Fusus al-Hikam* [Bezels of Wisdom] — represents a magistral synthesis of Sufi metaphysical and cosmological and spiritual teachings that previous masters had expressed only tangentially in their works. The voluminous nature of his literary production proves that by his day the Muslim esoterists were in need of great quantities of treatises, books, and commentaries in order to awaken a flickering intuition that in earlier times would have been satisfied with but a few words. Ibn 'Ata'illah lived to see the day when he would have to defend the teachings of Ibn al-'Arabi against the calumnies hurled at him by the Hanbalite theologian and canonist Ibn Taymiyyah (d. 1328). Those teachings of *wahdat al-wujud* would represent a definitive formulation of Sufi metaphysical positions and, along with his cosmological and other teachings, would be an intellectual heritage that Muslim esoterists turned to time and again as the centuries went by.

The second phenomenon of that century was the appearance, all over the Muslim world, of numerous Sufi orders. Both the Path in a generic sense and a Sufi order in a particular sense are called *tariqah*; previously, there had been "circles" (*tawa'if*) of Sufism, like the Salimiyyah of the 9th century, characterized by their small number of adherents; then, in the 12th century, one or two Sufi orders, like the Qadiriyyah, saw the light of day; but there had not previously been anything like the renascence of Sufism in the 13th century. The Mawlawiyyah, the Chishtiyyah, the Kubrawiyyah, the Ahmadiyyah, and the Shadhiliyyah, to name just a few of the important ones, were orders that drew vast numbers of Muslims into their midst, Muslims from all walks of life, from lowly peasants to highly placed public officials and even sultans and ministers and the religious chiefs of the state. These *tariqahs*, once established, continued to the present-day Muslim world without interruption, some of them spreading out over the entire Muslim world, with Shaykhs who did not even know one another but who shared a common linkage to the founding Shaykh of the order, who in turn was linked, master-by-master, to the Prophet of Islam. The Shadhilite Sufi order, to which Ibn 'Ata'illah belonged, spread far and wide, so that by his day it had numerous masters in Spain, Morocco, Algeria, Tunisia, Egypt, Syria, and Mecca in the Hijaz. He was not the only Shaykh of the order in his time; there were others, even in Egypt. But he seems to have had a certain central position— otherwise his name would not figure as third in the initiatic chain of transmission (*silsilah*), immediately after his own teacher's name, Shaykh Abu 'l-'Abbas al-Mursi, who died in 1288.

It is interesting to observe that Ibn al-'Arabi and the Sufi orders just mentioned constitute a powerful reaffirmation of Islamic gnosis, amounting to nothing less than the spiritual rebirth of Islam. This took place in the Muslim world at the very same moment that the Christian world in the West was abandoning its spiritual birthright, and more especially its Neoplatonist heritage, in favor of Aristotelianism, as represented by its scholastic partisans of the 13th century such as Thomas Aquinas (d. 1274), who was a contemporary of Shaykh Ibn 'Ata'illah. The last representative of Christian Neoplatonism in the late Middle Ages of the West was another contemporary of Ibn 'Ata'illah's, Meister Eckhart (d. ca. 1327), the great German mystical sage who lived to see his sapiential positions condemned by the Church as heretical. Just as Sufism, which reflects Islamic Neoplatonism, laid the groundwork for the future development of the spiritual life in Islam after the 13th century, so, similarly, Christian Aristotelianism led eventually, step by step, to the negation of the gnostic message imbedded in the Christian religion and to the rise of rationalism and the disintegration of the Christian world.

The Islamic rebirth would not have been so powerfully fruitful had it not been for the centuries-old integration of Sufi institutions into the fabric of Islamic society. Earlier rulers of Islam, especially the Saljuks, had built numerous *madrasahs*, or religious schools for instruction in Sunnite Islam, and *khanqahs*, which were the buildings where the Sufi Shaykhs imparted instruction to their disciples and watched over them in the contemplative cells. Later rulers, such as the Ayyubids and the Mamluks in Egypt and Syria, followed their example and built many *madrasahs* and *khanqahs*. They did this no doubt to strengthen the foundations of Sunnite Islam both exoterically and esoterically; many of the Muslim sultans were themselves disciples of Sufi Shaykhs and anxious to insure that they were housed in imposing structures. As a result, a kind of court protocol arose, which was applied to those masters of the Path recognized by the state as the official spokesmen for the Sufi adherents. These Shaykhs had special titles used to address them during court ceremonies or in correspondence; they held lofty ranks in the courts; the sultans and their retinues visited them regularly for advice and counsel; and the state provided the Shaykhs and their disciples with stipends and imposing quarters in the *khanqahs* built by the sultans. This was also another way of controlling the Sufi teachers and their disciples, and keeping them more or less in line with the ruling officials. The building of *khanqahs* by sultans was also an easy means of showing the public at large that the rulers were the champions of religion and its protectors. For this reason, many of the Shaykhs of Sufism stayed clear of the public officials, sultans, ministers, and lesser figures, so as not to be pressed into situations they could not control; and likewise, they never went near any of the public *khanqahs* (also called *zawiyahs*), preferring to teach in their own homes or in privately owned buildings. From this it can be seen that the public *khanqahs*, like the medieval Christian monasteries, could easily decline in the sense of increasing worldliness and preoccupation with material things; and decline they did, so much so that some of the Sufis fled from them as from the plague.

Long before Ibn 'Ata'illah came upon the scene, there was a general awareness among the people that the Shaykhs of the Path, together with their institutions, represented something quite distinct from the religious authorities of the Law, the *'ulama,'* who had their own social and religious institutions. An ambience had been created, in other words, that allowed everyone to find his level within the different layers of Islam, from the exoteric to the esoteric. Sufism was clearly visible everywhere, not merely because of its frequently imposing *khanqahs*, its public role, its literary and musical contributions, its political and economic power in the form of military fraternities and craft guilds, but also because of the presence of numerous saints, both men and women, who either lived in fixed abodes in the cities or else wandered about as mendicants, and who exerted a tremendous influence on the general populace. In view of all this, to consider Sufism as a kind of exotic mysticism confined to a few ecstatic Sufis who found themselves at cross-purposes with their fellow Muslims and who uttered strange sayings from time to time is really not to understand just how normal Sufism was in the traditional Islamic civilization. Very often, tens upon thousands of individuals belonged to the orders in one of the great cities. The person desirous of leading a contemplative life did not have to look far before he came into contact with Sufism or was led to it by circumstances. Although initially hostile to Sufism, Ibn

'Ata'illah changed his mind on the occasion of his first visit to Shaykh Abu 'l-'Abbas al-Mursi, who lived in Alexandria, not too far from his own home. He was not the only Sufi teacher there at the time; the others living there then also had numberless disciples. The tradition had crystallized long before the 13th century. It provided a ready-made mould for the aforementioned "second Revelation" of the Islamic faith, which was going on when Ibn 'Ata'illah grew up in Alexandria. He himself was influenced by the Sufi currents of the day: He knew the works of Ibn al-'Arabi, he belonged to the Shadhilite order and was one of its Shaykhs, and he moved within the prescribed institutional framework provided by the tradition that made his task as a Shaykh relatively simple to carry out, for he had nothing to invent from scratch. He was but one of scores of eminent Sufi Shaykhs in Egypt alone, let alone elsewhere in the Muslim world, all of whom had the backing of the rich institutional resources put at their disposal by the tradition as a whole.

Let us now turn to his life.

Very little is known of the early period in the life of Ibn 'Ata'illah, or even when he was born, though it can be said with some plausibility that his birth occurred around the year 1250. We do know that he was born into a distinguished family of Malikite religious scholars of Alexandria. His grandfather, who left behind some religious compositions of a certain merit, was either the founder or the reviver of a dynasty of scholars known as the Banu Ibn 'Ata'illah; and in the course of time Ibn 'Ata'illah himself became an eminent member of that dynasty and took the place of his grandfather in Alexandrian religious circles. His family originated among the Judham, an Arab tribe that settled in Egypt during the early Muslim conquests; hence Ibn 'Ata'illah had pure Arab ancestors in his background.

From an early age he was destined for greatness in Malikite studies. He had the best teachers in all the ancillary disciplines of the Law, such as grammar, the study of the *hadiths* of the Prophet, Qur'anic commentary, jurisprudence, theology, and Arabic literature. His expertness in Malikism—which is one of the most uniform schools of jurisprudence in Islam, especially in North Africa and formerly in Spain—soon drew attention to him, and knowledgeable Alexandrian scholars were not long in comparing him with his famous grandfather as a religious scholar. More than likely, he attended one of the religious schools that the Ayyubid sultans had constructed in Alexandria for the study of the Law, especially in its Malikite aspects.

Although Egypt had long been dominated by the Shafi'ite school of jurisprudence, Alexandria fell to the influence of Malikism, due in large measure to the location of the city as a crossroads between the eastern and western parts of the Muslim world bordering the Mediterranean. It had a sizable colony of North Africans who had settled there because of its congenial atmosphere, and with the passage of time the seaport took on a Malikite coloration and even a special North African culture. This explains the prevailing religious orientation of the Banu Ibn 'Ata'illah, whose Malikism came spontaneously from the transplanted North Africans and Andalucians living there. Moreover, apart from this question of Malikism, which has to do with exoteric Islam, there was also a special flower to the Sufism of Alexandria, for many of its teachers were really Moroccans or even Andalucians, who were either passing through or stopping there permanently. Some of the Alexandrian Sufis in the days of Ibn 'Ata'illah are among the most illustrious names that Sufism has to offer. The founder of the Shadhiliyyah, to mention one, spent the latter part of his life in one of the great towers then rising from the walls that surrounded the city. It was a well-equipped tower, with floors for his family, a mosque, the *zawiyah* where he gave instruction, and cells for meditation. The fact that Shaykh Abu 'l-Hasan ash-Shadhili saw fit to leave Morocco and, later, the city of Tunis and head for Alexandria shows something of the shift in the spiritual axis of the Muslim world. Previously, Sufism had started in the east and headed toward the west; now it was coming from the west and heading east. This had become quite noticeable in the days of Ibn al-'Arabi, who had left Andalucia for countries in the eastern Mediterranean region, finally settling down in Damascus, where he died. The reversal of Sufi movement pointed to the fact that the western part of the Muslim world had become a bastion of Sufism that would influence many parts of the Muslim world from then on.

Shaykh Abu 'l-Hasan ash-Shadhili had originally founded his order in the city of Tunis in the year 1227, where it had great success; then, as a result of a vision commanding him to move eastward, he moved the center of his order to Alexandria in the year 1244, six years from the probable date of Ibn 'Ata'illah's birth. In both Alexandria and Cairo, Abu 'l-Hasan ash-Shadhili had enormous success, not only among the ordinary people, but also among the ruling classes. His *tariqah* has been characterized as a throwback to the days of the Prophet and his companions because its adepts wore no distinctive garments setting them apart from the world around them nor did they abandon their professions or trades in society to take up a life of mendicancy, as did many of the other Sufi orders. Shaykh Abu 'l-Hasan taught his disciples to lead the life of contemplation while still in the world; he even disliked initiating any would-be disciple unless that person already had a profession or trade. In this respect, the Shaykh resembled the Prophet, who taught his companions the doctrine of Islam but did not demand of them that they quit their posts in the world; quite the contrary, they were to bring the principles of Islam into their life in the world and transform their existence. It is not surprising, then, that Shaykh Abu 'l-Hasan himself was sometimes misunderstood by the authorities of the state because they did not see on him the usual Sufi garments, nor did he have the attitudes that go with the wandering mendicant or the ascetic or devotee.

Gnosis was the perspective of his order. He insisted, as had previous Sufis, that the gnostics took precedence over the ascetics and devotees, which is not to say that his order had no ascetical or devotional elements. The gnosis he speaks of is really the simple type that one finds in early Islam, without any of the complicated analytical scaffolding that one finds in the works of Ibn al-'Arabi; it is a gnosis that arises from an ardent faith and not from mental gymnastics of a conceptual nature. As a matter of fact, he wrote nothing in the way of a detailed and schematic presentation of his doctrines. All we have from his hand are the widely recited litanies, with such names as "The Litany of the Ocean," "The Litany of Light," "The Litany of Victory," and so on, for which he claimed divine inspiration. These litanies are Qur'anic verses interlaced with his own words and contain rather powerful variations on the theme of the divine Unity. They were immensely popular in the days of Ibn 'Ata'illah and are still chanted today. If we go by what Ibn 'Ata'illah says, they functioned as meditational recitations for the Shadhilite initiates, who used them at different moments during the course of the day.

We know that the father of Ibn 'Ata'illah was a disciple of Shaykh Abu 'l-Hasan ash-Shadhili, for Ibn 'Ata'illah got a good deal of his biographical information on the Shaykh from his father; but we have no reason to believe that Ibn 'Ata'illah himself ever met or saw the founder of the Shadhiliyyah. Even if he had met him or seen him, he would have been much too young—no more than five or six years of age—to profit from the experience. Shaykh Abu'l-Hasan ash-Shadhili died in the eastern desert of Egypt in the year 1258, several weeks after the Mongols had sacked the city of Baghdad and brought the 'Abbasid Caliphate to an end. His shrine in that part of the desert stands to the present day.

Shortly before his death, he designated as his successor over the order the Andalucian Abu 'l-'Abbas al-Mursi (d. 1288), who had joined his circle of disciples in Tunis and accompanied him to Alexandria, remaining by his side till his death. Al-Mursi took as his residence the same tower that had been used by his master, and remained there till his death, never leaving Alexandria. Unlike his teacher, who seemed to be on good terms with the political leaders and authorities of the day, al-Mursi never had easy relations with the local governors or provincial or even higher chiefs; he refused to have anything whatsoever to do with them, and would remain stonily silent whenever they came to visit him. This betokened a much harsher attitude on his part, whereas his teacher appears to have been more easygoing. Like his master, he wrote nothing at all, but he also left behind some litanies, which are not as powerful or as well known as those of his teacher. What we know about him is due largely to the biographical work of his disciple Ibn 'Ata'illah, but this is really a compilation of quotations of a Sufi nature derived from al-Mursi and ash-Shadhili, with some rather sparse details about their lives. Even so, the greatness of al-Mursi comes through in the quotations; however, we do not need Ibn 'Ata'illah to prove that greatness, for a number of al-Mursi's contemporaries, whether Sufis or not, have left behind in their own works their observations on his saintly and wise nature. By the time of his death, the number of masters of the Shadhilite order in North Africa, Spain, Egypt, and other places must have been quite high. We know the names of many of them, and when we consider that they all had numerous disciples, the influence of this one order alone in the Muslim world must have been considerable by the time Ibn 'Ata'illah took over as a Shaykh in Cairo.

Curiously, Ibn 'Ata'illah was not drawn to the Path in his youth, and did not then follow the example of his father, who had been a disciple of ash-Shadhili and probably also of al-Mursi. Instead, he plunged into his studies as a religious scholar and became something of a prodigy, gaining a certain renown even though he was youthful. His fellow students had warned him that anyone who delved into Sufism would not get far in his studies of the Law, and never master it. He followed their advice and added to it a strange hostility toward the Sufi Path and an even stranger hostility, which he was hard put to explain, toward Shaykh Abu 'l-'Abbas al-Mursi himself. Violent arguments had occasionally taken place between him and some of the Shaykh's disciples, and he had said to them that beyond the letter of the Law there is nothing else to seek. Having nothing specific against the Shaykh, his hostility remained rather vague and diffused; but he finally mustered enough courage to go to one of the Shaykh's public talks on the different aspects of Sufism. This was Ibn 'Ata'illah's first view of the Shaykh, and it took place in the year 1276, some twelve years before the master's death, which means that he was a disciple of his for that period of time. That first visit proved to be the decisive turning point in his life, for he was converted to Sufism right there and he forthwith put himself under the Shaykh's guidance and became in time one of his most serious and promising disciples, joyfully learning that his entry into the Path was not considered by his teacher to be incompatible with his studies of the Law. The Shaykh even predicted that Ibn 'Ata'illah would become an authority in both the Path and the Law—a prediction that eventually came true.

The metamorphosis of a Malikite religious scholar into a Sufi Shaykh is not easily discernible from his writings, but it is clear that it could not have been too many years after his first meeting with his Shaykh. For one thing, he wrote his *Kitab al-Hikam*, which shows mastery of the Path, while his teacher was still alive, since we hear that al-Mursi gave the book his stamp of approval; for another, he was already established in Cairo as a Shaykh when al-Mursi died in Alexandria in 1288. It was thus in Cairo that al-Mursi's prediction of greatness for Ibn

'Ata'illah came true, for there he spent the remainder of his life as an honored and well-known Sufi teacher and a Malikite religious scholar. He led two lives, as it were: One was his professional life as a teacher of Malikite studies in various public institutions and mosques in Cairo (such as the Azhar and the newly built Mansuriyyah complex) plus his public preaching, which drew large audiences; the other life was devoted to his duties as a Shaykh of the Shadhilite order, but we are not sure where in Cairo his *zawiyah* might have been. We know for certain that he had disciples in both Cairo and Alexandria, and one of the historians of the day pictures him as being the spokesman for the Sufi adherents of the capital. He moved about in the Mamluk court, for he counseled the ill-starred Sultan al-Mansur Lajin (d. 1298) on religious manners. It is difficult to reconstruct his life in any detailed fashion, but, for the most part, it seems to have been rather uneventful.

Toward the end of his life, Ibn 'Ata'illah did have an unpleasant experience with one of the doctors of the Law who incarnated a certain puritanical and fundamentalist exoterism of Hanbalite persuasion. This was Ibn Taymiyyah, the theologian and jurist who died in Syria in 1328 after a long life of opposition to some of the great Sufis of Islamic history and active campaigning against such practices as visits to saints' tombs. He opposed such Sufi figures as Ibn al-'Arabi, whose writings he considered pantheistic, and had gotten himself into deep trouble with Sufi personalities in Cairo as a result of his attacks on the teachings of *ash-Shaykh al-Akbar*, resulting in great commotion. Political and theological problems intervened to render the whole question even more complicated: The Hanbalites had always been a tiny school of jurisprudence, always known for its championship of nonspeculative theological dogmas that the other schools of jurisprudence preferred explaining through the use of speculative theology. Egypt was mostly a Shafi'ite country, and the Shafi'ites of the epoch, whether in Egypt or Syria, were largely of Ash'arite theological persuasion, which permitted them to explain some of the articles of faith through the use of rational argumentation in defense of religion. For centuries, the Shafi'ites and the Hanbalites had been at loggerheads with one another over such matters. Now came yet another opportunity for the Shafi'ites to suppress the Hanbalites, as Ibn Taymiyyah launched his attacks against some of the great names of Sufism. The confusion was compounded by the political personalities of the day among the Mamluk princes, who were then jockeying for power, and who saw, in the fluctuations of the verbal battles, great opportunities to advance their cause, depending on whether they were on the side of Ibn Taymiyyah or that of his antagonists. The whole matter came to a head when Shaykh Ibn 'Ata'illah, at the head of a long stream of Sufi Shaykhs and hundreds of their disciples, made his way through the narrow streets of Cairo to the Citadel, where the confrontation with Ibn Taymiyyah would take place. There, under the watchful eyes of the Egyptian religious authorities, who feared the power of Ibn Taymiyyah's puritanical ideas and his hold on certain sectors of the population, a futile discussion ensued between the Sufi Shaykh, representing Islamic esoterism, and the Hanbalite theologian, representing an extreme version of fundamentalist exoterism, with the result that the former withdrew with unpleasant memories of this stern and hidebound exponent of Hanbalism. That was the end of the matter, as far as he was concerned. He never mentioned Ibn Taymiyyah by name in any of his works, but it was clearly in reference to him that he warns the reader about the shallow-minded doctors of Islamic exoterism. As for Ibn Taymiyyah, it is one of the ironies of history that, like many of the *'ulama'* of his day, he belonged to one of the Sufi orders. This was not in the least unusual, given the great expansion in the ranks of the Sufi orders with the passage of time; but it did mean that

Sufism harbored in its midst not only pure contemplative esoterists, but also a great number of individuals who were not spiritually fit for the higher reaches of the Path and who interpreted it according to the limitations of their own mental horizons. If to that one added a certain fundamentalism and literalism, a pugnacious spirit, and even a persecution complex (which the Hanbalites had developed as a consequence of their championship of nonspeculative Islamic theology), then Ibn Taymiyyah's case can be easily understood, all the more in that he cultivated an air of reforming the Islamic tradition by harking back to the early days of the religion and eradicating everything that blocked the reaffirmation of primitive Islam.

Two years or so after the confrontation with Ibn Taymiyyah, the Shaykh died at about the age of sixty in the *madrasah* of the Mansuriyyah, where he had been teaching Malikite jurisprudence. His funeral procession to the Qarafah cemetery has been described as immense. His tomb still stands next to that of another Shadhilite saint, the famous Shaykh 'Ali Abu 'l-Wafa' (d. 1405), whose spiritual lineage connects him to Ibn 'Ata'illah. For centuries his tomb was famous and, like that of other Sufis' tombs, soon became the object of visits by pious Muslims and the focus of miraculous and charismatic phenomena. We are told by one of the historians of the time that Shaykh Ibn 'Ata'illah's person was characterized by an impressive majesty, which is not difficult to imagine for anyone who has read his works in Arabic, most of which are still circulating in printed editions at the present day.

The immediate legacy of the Shaykh is more concretely embodied in his disciples than in his books, for they relived under his guidance the truths contained in the Path, just as he had done previously under his own teacher. They are therefore the links that connect him with subsequent generations, and this is especially true of those who became spiritual masters in their turn, thus prolonging the inner life of the order and perpetuating it in time and space. His direct successor in the Shadhilite order, if we go by a *silsilah* that is common in North Africa and Egypt, was Shaykh Dawud al-Bakhili (d. 1332), who was likewise a learned Malikite scholar. His major work, entitled *'Uyun al-haqa'iq* [The Sources of Esoteric Truths], exists only in manuscript form, though sizable extracts from it can be found in later Sufi works. Another eminent disciple was Shaykh Shihab ad-Din ibn Maylaq (d. 1349), a preacher and transmitter of *hadiths* who became well known as a Shaykh of Sufism in his day. Among the religious scholars of the day who were disciples of Ibn 'Ata'illah mention should be made of the great Shafi'ite theologian and canonist Taqi ad-Din as-Subki (d. 1355), who always held his master in deep reverence and maintained a profound respect for all the Sufis. He is an example of the numerous religious authorities of Islam throughout the centuries who have known that Sufism embodies the spiritual life of the religion, and that the saintly teachers possess a spiritual authority transcending the merely religious authority of the *'ulama'*. We often hear that the opponents of Sufism have come mostly from the ranks of the religious chiefs and scholars envious of the love shown the Sufi saints and sages by the people. But this is to forget that, from the very beginning, when the two dimensions of Islam separated into esoteric and exoteric, there have always been religious authorities who recognized their limitations and who knew that the Path (*tariqah*) and the Law (*shari'ah*) issued from the same Revelation and that the Path was synonymous with Sufism.

The Works of Ibn 'Ata'illah

The Sufis have produced a rather impressive spiritual literature throughout the centuries, not only in Arabic, but also in Persian and Turkish, these being the three principal Islamic tongues. Some Sufis have left behind literally hundreds of works on esoterism; we have only to think of Ibn al-'Arabi, who is easily the most prolific sage of both the East and the West, to see just how vast Sufi literary production can be. Few of the Sufi works have been translated into Western languages; the rest lie buried in manuscript libraries or are circulated in printed editions in the East. It is a characteristic of the Islamic religion, with its bifurcation into an esoteric and exoteric aspect, that the Sufi works have always coexisted alongside the standard works on Islamic exoterism, and that many Muslims, not necessarily belonging to the Sufi orders, would read both types of literature.

While Ibn 'Ata'illah was not a prolific author, he did write works on Sufism that have endured throughout the centuries, perhaps because he was the first of the early Shadhilite masters to set down on paper the teachings of the order. Perhaps by training, perhaps by talent, it was left to him, among the Shadhilite masters of the day, to write down the teachings of the order with real authority. Other Shadhilite masters contemporaneous with him never saw fit to write anything at all, which is not unusual in Sufism, but as time went by, all of this changed and a spate of books and treatises came from the Shaykhs right down to our time. In that stream of literature, it is an indication of his worth and importance that the major works of Ibn 'Ata'illah have always held their own as authoritative summations of the Path. Nowadays, they are published and republished regularly, indicating that they are in considerable demand. This is especially so for his principal work, *Kitab al-Hikam*, which will be analyzed later on. It was immediately successful and has always been highly appreciated for its aphoristic presentation of the truths of the Path.

Next in importance to the *Kitab al-Hikam* in his book *Miftah al-Falah wa Misbah al-Arwah* [The Key of Success and the Lamp of Spirits], a concise and comprehensive exposition of the Sufi method of Invocation (*dhikr*). It is perhaps the first work in

Sufism that gives the general and particular technical aspects of this exceedingly important Sufi method of spiritual concentration through the use of a divine Name of the Divinity. Previous works on Sufism had given a chapter or so to the *dhikr*, but his is the first whole book to be devoted to it. A short work, the *Miftah* is written in a lucid Arabic style replete with citations drawn from the Qur'an and the *hadiths*, not to mention the early Sufis, and was probably composed in the last decade of his life. Quite popular in present-day Sufi circles, it has often been reprinted.

A companion piece to the *Hikam* is his *Kitab at-Tanwir fi isqat at-Tadbir* [Light on the Elimination of Self-Direction], which is a simple and clear presentation of the Shadhilite approach to the virtues, such as patience, sincerity, hope, love, fear. They are all seen as contained in a single, all-embracing virtue, that of "the elimination of self-direction" (*isqat at-Tadbir*); and once this egocentric self-direction goes, the divine direction takes over. The book ends in a series of intimate discourses of rare beauty on the matter of self-direction. Since the work contains a reference to a great Tunisian Sufi whom the author knew, followed by the usual formula for the deceased, we may conclude that it was written in the last decade or so of his life, the Tunisian having died some ten years before Ibn 'Ata'illah's death in 1309. The book abounds with citations from the statements of the first two masters of the Shadhiliyyah, and on this score alone is quite important.

His biographical work, *Kitab al-Lata'if fi Manaqib Abi 'l-'Abbas al-Mursi wa Shaykhihi Abi 'l-Hasan* [The Subtle Blessings in the Saintly Lives of Abu 'l-'Abbas al-Mursi and His Master Abu'l-Hasan], is not so much a reconstruction of their lives as it is a record of what they said on different aspects of the Path. It is somewhat autobiographical in that it has numerous references to the religious and Sufi notables who were the contemporaries of Ibn 'Ata'illah. Because it transmits the words of the first two masters of the order, who never wrote any books themselves, the work has always been highly esteemed as one of the basic sources for the early history of the Shadhiliyyah. Not only that, without this work it would be practically impossible to write more than a few lines on the life of Shaykh Ibn 'Ata'illah himself. All future works of Shadhilite masters make numerous references to the *Lata'if* when they cite the words of the first two Shaykhs of the order. Written in straightforward Arabic prose, it contains numerous litanies composed by the first two Shaykhs and others; it seems to be among the last of his books.

His small book *al-Qasd al-Mujarrad fi Ma'rifat al-Ism al-Mufrad* [The Pure Goal Concerning Knowledge of the Unique Name], written also in a sober but powerful style, sets out the doctrine on the supreme Name, *Allah*, both in itself, as a means of concentration, and in relation to the other "beautiful Names" of the Divinity, as the Qur'an calls the ninety-nine Names of *Allah*, which are often chanted by Muslims with the help of rosaries or otherwise. A rather profound metaphysical theory underlies his explanation of the Names, the whole showing that the Shadhilites had spiritual and intellectual doctrines of a high order. It is difficult to say when this work was composed.

While his other works are of minor importance, one of them, the *Taj al-'Arus al-Hawi li-Tahdhib an-Nufus* [The Bride's Crown Containing the Discipline of the Soul], still seems to be popular enough. It is made up largely of extracts drawn from his *Hikam*, *Tanwir*, and *Lata'if*, and this rather eclectic nature may be the reason why it has been popular. Lacking any interior unity, it might have been put together by him as a memory aid or as a brief synthesis of his other works. Very likely, it is one of the last things he wrote.

Ibn 'Ata'illah's remaining compositions, such as his *'Unwan at-Tawfiq fi Adab at-Tariq* [The Sign of Success Concerning the Discipline of the Path], a gloss on a poem by the famous Andalucian Shaykh Abu Madyan (d. 1197) on the relations between master and disciple, are less well known. Of his lost works, we have only the titles. It is clear, however, that we have in hand today the best and most famous of his writings.

The Legacy of Shaykh Ibn 'Ata'illah

Ibn 'Ata'illah inherited from his own master, Shaykh Abu 'l-'Abbas al-Mursi, the living tradition of Sufism, which has nothing bookish about it, but is instead a kind of "presence" transmitted by the authentic masters who expound its nature to their disciples, or to those who have the right receptivity, and give them the means of reaching the Real. This is why some of the Sufis have said that Sufism is not to be found in books, which represent, after all, only verbalized or conceptualized reflections of a vast ocean of Reality that the masters have experienced and teach their disciples to experience through the love and knowledge of that Reality. Ibn 'Ata'illah, through the wisdom, sanctity, and grace of his teacher, al-Mursi, achieved spiritual realization of the Absolute that the Islamic tradition names *Allah*. The term "Sufi" really means, in the strict application made of it by the Sufis themselves, the one who has reached the end of the Path; everyone else is called *faqir*, or some such word. At a certain moment before his master's death, Ibn 'Ata'illah became a Sufi in that rigorous sense; but, in addition to that, he also received authority to teach the Path to others as a Shaykh; and we can only imagine that the authority must come ultimately from a celestial source, for it is not given to any man — as man — to give himself the authority to teach others how to reach God. This was the first, and the most important, legacy that Shaykh Ibn 'Ata'illah left behind: He taught others the Path, and there emerged under his tutelage some exceptional individuals who in turn became teachers. Thus, the tradition he received was transmitted to others, and those among them who had the proper realization transmitted it in their turn. This, from the Sufi viewpoint, was his crucial role; all else was secondary.

As regards his literary works, they represent his second legacy and have an importance, historically speaking, of their own. He was the first of the early masters of the Shadhiliyyah to write books, and he was close enough to the beginning period of the order so that things were still fresh and could be witnessed firsthand. Because he had a gift for summing up, in clear and simple fashion, the main theses of Sufi spirituality, his works have a perennial value. His style, together with the ring of authority in his words, has drawn many seekers of the Path to his books.

Shaykh Ibn 'Ata'illah did not address his works, it would seem, only to those individuals who had withdrawn from society to live a life of reclusive meditation, nor to those who lived in the world but were contemplatives; instead, he addressed both. It is important to remember that the founder of the Shadhiliyyah wanted his disciples to work in the world, not to leave it for a life of mendicancy. In his days, Ibn 'Ata'illah saw armies of ascetics and other wandering groups of devotees moving through the big cities under the leadership of gaunt-looking chiefs. Not that the ascetics always moved about in vast numbers; there were isolated individuals as well. But the fact is that many of the Sufi orders also contributed to the general movement by advocating a life of wandering. While Sufism in no wise can be reduced to asceticism or devotionalism, it is nevertheless true that things had reached a point, in the history of Sufism, where a kind of insistence that the Path is also for those living in the world was necessary. If Sufism had developed, over the centuries, rather impressive institutions in the midst of society, distinctive garments and other appurtenances of dress, attitudes of withdrawal from the worldly society of their times, and the like, then a remanifestation of the way things were in the days of the Prophet was a distinct possibility, just waiting for someone like Shaykh Abu 'l-Hasan to come along. Later on, at certain periods, the Shadhilite order would espouse the usual garments and other things associated with Sufism; but there seems always to have been a current of Shadhilism that kept itself far removed from such practices and insisted that the Path can be lived as it was in the time of Muhammad—without distinctive dress setting one group apart from the others, without withdrawing from one's professional activities in the midst of society, and without having to engage in a life of wandering. The early success of Shaykh Abu 'l-Hasan's order proves that his vision of things was right and that the spiritual transformation of society was possible without exaggerated asceticism and the abandonment of one's life in the world.

Introductory Remarks on the Kitab al-Hikam

Of all the works written by Ibn 'Ata'illah, the *Hikam* is certainly the most admired by later generations. References to it as a "book" in his other writings, or citations of this or that aphorism, prove his authorship. He evidently dictated the *Hikam* to one of his disciples, perhaps commenting on the meaning of its contents as he went along. This disciple was none other than the distinguished Shafi'ite jurist Taqi ad-Din as-Subki (d. 1355), a number of whose works on jurisprudence still circulate in the Muslim world, especially his juridical opinions that have the force of precedence. Later on, the Shadhilite master Ahmad Zarruq (d. 1493), a Moroccan Sufi who commented on the *Hikam*, received five of the works of Ibn 'Ata'illah, including the *Hikam*, from the historian as-Sakhawi (d. 1497), who also gave him the correct oral transmission, beginning with the previously mentioned Taqi ad-Din as-Subki.

The *Hikam* was written somewhere between 1276, when Ibn 'Ata'illah met his master for the first time, and the death of his master in 1288. It is more than likely that the *Hikam* was his first work, and one might look upon it as the fruit of his spiritual realization, or in any case as the expression of it in literary form. Sufism tends to scorn those individuals who write on spiritual matters without authority, and he himself mentions that all-important matter in chapter 20 of his *Hikam*. We may conclude, therefore, that the work reflects his role as a master of the Path and one fully empowered to speak with authority. The work itself, by the forcefulness of its expressions and the profundity of its convictions, leaves no doubt as to the author's magistracy in the Path. The Sufi Shaykh Ibn 'Ajibah (d. 1809), citing the great founder of the Darqawa branch of the Shadhiliyyah, Mawlay al-'Arabi ad-Darqawi (d. 1823), has the latter saying: "I heard the jurist al-Bannani say, 'The *Hikam* of Ibn 'Ata' is almost a revelation. Were it permitted to recite the daily ritual prayer without the Qur'an, the words of the *Hikam* would be allowed?'" One cannot grasp the full import of such a remark without knowing in advance that the Qur'an alone is considered to be a divine Revelation; the Sufis who claim for particular works a divine origin do not speak of Revelation but rather of inspiration, which is of lesser degree.

The term *hikam* is the plural of *hikmah*, which means "wisdom," "aphorism," "maxim," "gnome," among other meanings. Books with titles similar to Ibn Ata'illah's *Kitab al-Hikam* are by no means rare in Arabic literature—the Arabic language, with its rhythmic concision, lends itself easily and gracefully to gnomic expression. The relationship between hikmah and *ma'rifah* is rather evident; both imply a profound knowledge, in this case an experiential and concrete knowledge of the Real (*al-Haqq*) that infinitely transcends the abstract and purely mental aspects of what is usually called "knowledge."

INTRODUCTION

Gnosis does have a theoretical aspect to it. When we strip it of its realizational nature, what remains is precisely the doctrinal or conceptual residue in the mind. But here too there is a difference between this and the purely rationalistic approach to knowledge, for the concepts of the gnostics of Sufism flow directly into their reasoning or discursive mind from the source of intellections in their heart. Ibn 'Ata'illah could just as easily have entitled his work *Kitab al-Ma'rifah* [The Book of Gnosis], for that basically is what it deals with, a gnosis that is at once both theoretical doctrine and realizational application.

The *Hikam* has been the object of numerous commentaries by other Sufi Shaykhs, who have seen in the work a sort of condensed version of the Path. Generally, the commentators have been of the Shadhilite line; as a result, a certain homogeneity results, and this makes for an easier comprehension of the work inasmuch as the technical terminology in it is constantly repeated. Moreover, his other books, such as the *Tanwir*, the *Miftah*, and the *Lata'if*, open up still further angles of insight, until the *Hikam* itself, properly understood and assimilated, ends by being its own best commentary.

The phrase "And he said (may God be pleased with him!)" crops up repeatedly in the text, and is considered by all as part and parcel of the received text. Obviously, it is not of the author's composition, since it is a phrase that is standard for a deceased person in Islam. How to account for it? Shaykh Ahmad Zarruq prefers to explain its presence in the work as a result of the different dictating sessions, the disciple marking off the beginning of each session with the phrase in question, after having heard the explanation given by the author on the contents of the previous session. This seems to be the most satisfactory way of accounting for the phrase in the text.

The *Hikam* is divisible into three principal parts: the aphorisms, the treatises, and the supplications or intimate discourses. The aphorisms or maxims are the substance of the work, so much so that the last two parts could almost be relegated to one side. In strict sense, it is only the first part that should be called by the name of *hikam*, or aphorisms. These are short, pithy maxims in felicitous Arabic prose that is often rhymed. Individually, they can be separated from one another by their content, or they can be loosely grouped together under some dominant theme; otherwise, they stand and fall as they are, succeeding one another in a circular sequence that seems not to have, at first glance, any logical order, though there is a unity that emerges after a while. That unity in the text is supplied by the overall radiance of gnosis, which holds everything together. The internal structure of the *Hikam* is such that it can be likened to a necklace of precious jewels, the necklace itself being the *ma'rifah* in question; but in the course of centuries, particular aphorisms have gained a certain renown, a kind of independence, appearing time and again in different Sufi works that cite them because of their inimitable aptness. As for the gnosis itself, it revolves around the metaphysical postulate in the Islamic doctrine of *tawhid* ("the affirmation of the Oneness of God") that the One can have no associates of any kind: *Allah* is the Absolute, the Real, the Infinite, the Eternal; nothing else can be that way and must instead be relative, unreal, finite, transitory, depending on our perspective or point of departure. Profound spiritual consequences flow from this doctrine of *tawhid*, which is fundamental to Islam and therefore to Sufism, which takes *tawhid* to its vanishing point in the Absolute.

In passing, one must say that Ibn 'Ata'illah, like others in his epoch, was marked by the scholastic terminology of Ash'arite theology, which he studied under one of its great exponents. He was thus a Malikite jurist of Ash'arite persuasion. But one must not be deceived by epithets: He was first and foremost a Sufi gnostic and only secondarily a theologian. There is thus a difference in planes of reference, which must not be lost sight of when pondering his theses: Gnosis must not be reduced to theology or philosophy, and he would be the first to say as much.

The aphorisms are not numbered by the author. One could, and one should, number them by way of bringing out their independent existence and defining their contours. That is what has been done in the translation, making the total of aphorisms 262 in all. In addition, some commentators have perceived a kind of grouping of thoughts in the *Hikam*. Wherever the phrase "And he said (may God be pleased with him!)" occurs, these commentators think that they discern a kind of break in the subject matter, a new train of thought about to take place. While such a phrase might have occurred in step with the different periods of dictation, as mentioned previously, it is nevertheless true that prolonged acquaintance with the *Hikam* induces in the reader the impression that a particular coloration of thought dominates each section or "chapter." It is no doubt this dominance that has resulted in the division of the work into twenty-five chapters. This division is traditional, and has been maintained in the translation.

While numerous previous Shaykhs of Sufism have composed similarly aphoristic works, no other has had so lasting an effect as Ibn 'Ata'illah, at least of those writing in Arabic. Why so? Perhaps the answer lies in the combination of profound Sufi teachings and real charm of language that characterizes the *Hikam*. It not only unfolds the integral Sufi doctrine on the spiritual life, but it does so in a manner calculated to appeal to all pious and knowledgeable Muslims. The powerful and yet gracious union of thought and language makes of the *Hikam* a memorizable work of universal appeal, and it is perhaps this that sets it apart from all other works of similar nature.

After the aphorisms comes the second part of the work in the form of four short treatises written by the author in response to questions posed to him by his disciples. They are couched in a straighforward Arabic style and seem, at least initially, to have been appended to the aphorisms by another hand. But this impression is soon negated by the feeling that they form a welcome interlude between the concise structure of the aphorisms and the equally brief supplications or intimate discourses that end the work. In other words, after a long series of aphorisms calling for maximum concentration of mind, the tension is broken by the expansive character of the treatises.

The third and last part of the *Hikam* returns us once again to brief formulations, this time in the guise of supplications or "intimate conversations" (*munajat*) addressed to the Divinity in confidential fashion. More often than not, they are paradoxical questions asked of God. Total submission and poverty of spirit on the part of the servant addressing his Lord are the main themes of these discourses. Coming after the aphorisms, which have a shock value in their actual form, and the treatises, which release the pent-up tension generated by the aphorisms, the supplications depict the state of the soul that has found its Center and is receptively open to Heaven and now on intimate terms with the Creator. The contemplative has at last found the eye of the storm in the central axis of his being and is now in a state of peace and serenity; the questions and paradoxical exclamations are really for the sake of others, not for himself. This seems a fitting end to the work.

As stated, the aphorisms have been given numbers in the translation. This docs no particular violence to them, since the numbering is only to delineate what seem to be complete thoughts. The numbering herein reaches 262; but Shaykh 'Abd al-Majid ash-Sharnubi (d. 1904), one of the commentators, tells us that he counted 264 aphorisms, yet in his commentary he makes no use of numbers; perhaps others would number them differently. Be that as it may, and by way of summing up what lies ahead, there are 262 aphorisms spread out over 25 chapters, 4 treatises, and 34 intimate discourses.

INTRODUCTION

Texts and Commentaries

In the translation of the *Hikam* that follows, a number of texts, both in published and printed forms, together with their commentaries, have been used. The *Hikam* is remarkably well preserved, due no doubt to its importance as a major Sufi work. There are of course variant readings, but these are of minor importance and in no way affect the integrity of the text as a whole. Published versions can have typographical mistakes—the contrary would be unusual—and the manuscript version might occasionally be vowelized incorrectly by an inattentive scribe, but such minor imperfections can easily be overcome.

For the text of the *Hikam*, the following manuscripts have been used: (1) MS Escorial, no. 763, and (2) MS Escorial, no. 786. They will serve to control the published texts, which can be found in numerous versions at the present day, often with a commentary; the *Iqaz al-Himam*, a widely used gloss on the *Hikam* by Ibn 'Ajibah, is the published text (found at the end of the commentary) that we use here.

Numerous commentaries on the *Hikam* have been produced over the centuries by different Sufi Shaykhs, most of them Shadhilite or else inspired by Shadhilism, although the work is universal and not confined to one order. It is difficult to say when the earliest commentary might have been written. Some, dating back to authors who lived in the 14th century, are still available in manuscript libraries. The commentary by Shaykh Ibn 'Abbad ar-Rundi (d. 1390) is quite famous and often reprinted today; for that reason, we have followed its explanations of certain texts of the *Hikam* from time to time. The second commentary we have relied on is the seventeenth of some thirty commentaries written by the Shadhilite master Shaykh Ahmad Zarruq (d. 1493), who is one of the Sufis figuring in the chain of transmission of the Shadhiliyyah that passes through Shaykh Ibn 'Ata'illah. Most of his commentaries on the *Hikam* remain in manuscript form; they were written as the author moved from Fez eastward through North Africa to Egypt to Lebanon, and then back again to Fez. The seventeenth has recently been published and is thus easily accessible. But we have relied on two manuscripts containing his commentaries: MS Escorial, no. 738, which is his fifteenth commentary, written in Bougie, in present-day Algeria; and MS Escorial, no. 776, a very important one, given that it is an autograph copy. Since Shaykh Ahmad Zarruq claimed to have received the *Hikam* through a correct line of transmission going back to Ibn 'Ata'illah, the text imbedded in the autograph has a special authority as far as authenticity is concerned. Other commentators we have consulted are: Shaykh 'Abd Allah ash-Sharqawi, whose commentary is on the margin of the published text with gloss by Ibn 'Abbad ar-Rundi; and Shaykh 'Abd al-Majid ash-Sharnubi, whose commentary is on the margin of his own gloss on a Sufi poem.

In our own explanatory notes to the *Hikam*, due care has been given to the author's doctrine as expounded in his other works, which very often spell out in greater detail what is condensed in a single aphorism. We have to remember that Sufism is a long-standing tradition: There is not only the Qur'an to be taken into account but also the *hadiths* of the Prophet and the remarks of the early contemplative ascetics of Islam; then, on the basis of that, one must pay attention to the writings of the early Sufis, great and small, and the later figures; and finally, within each Sufi order—especially after the 13th century—there is an additional mass of literature and interpretive texts, not to mention original compositions, and the all-important "oral tradition" (let us not forget to mention the living words of the Sufi master) which must be taken into consideration when seeking to understand the place of a work like the *Hikam* and the meaning of its words. Sufism surfaced as a name—not a reality, for that was already in the Revelation—some one thousand and two hundred years ago. It has thus had over a thousand years of uninterrupted existence to develop a rather formidable technical vocabulary that makes its concepts easy enough to understand for those who have the intuitive perception and are willing to give the time and the effort. The vocabulary of the *Hikam* is not in the least novel, except for a few terms here and there that characterize the Shadhiliyyah. The best way to assimilate the meaning of those terms is to head straight to one of the traditional authorities—the commentators, whose role in Islam, as in other religions, is to explain scriptural and other texts for later generations without betraying their spirit. Three commentators' names crop up frequently in the notes to the *Hikam*, and all of them have the advantage of looking at the text through the eyes of spiritual masters, which is what they were. The first one in point of time is the already-mentioned Shaykh Ibn 'Abbad ar-Rundi (d. 1390), from Ronda, in Spain, when Andalucia was still Islamic. The second is Shaykh Ahmad Zarruq (d. 1493), a learned scholar born in Fez, who traveled a great deal in the eastern Muslim world. And the third is also the latest in point of time: Shaykh Ibn 'Ajibah (d. 1809), a remarkable Moroccan Sufi master, who participated in the extraordinary spiritual flowering that took place in the early 19th century under the direction of the great Sufi saint and sage Shaykh Mawlay al-'Arabi ad-Darqawi (d. 1823). That entire renascence would have continuous repercussions right into the 20th century, when still another great master—perhaps one of the greatest in the entire history of Sufism—flourished, Shaykh Ahmad al-'Alawi, about whom Martin Lings has written an important work, *A Sufi Saint of the Twentieth Century*. All of these individuals read and pondered the *Hikam* of Shaykh Ibn 'Ata'illah, not as if they were reading the words of some isolated genius who suddenly appeared without relation to his past, but in the full awareness that they were examining the fruits of a man who had realized in himself spiritually the truths of the contemplative Path of Islam and had put down, for the sake of others, his observations and instructions so that they might be emboldened to tread the Path toward *Allah*, the One without a second.

Ibn 'Ata'illah

The Book of Wisdom

(*Kitab al-Hikam*)

Chapter 1

He said (may God be pleased with him!):

1
One of the signs of relying on one's own deeds
is the loss of hope when a downfall occurs.[1]

2
Your desire for isolation,[2]
even though God has put you in the world to gain a living,
is a hidden passion.
And your desire to gain a living in the world,
even though God has put you in isolation,
is a comedown from a lofty aspiration.[3]

3
Antecedent intentions
cannot pierce the walls of predestined Decrees.[4]

4
Rest yourself from self-direction,
for what Someone Else has carried out on your behalf
you must not yourself undertake to do it.[5]

5
Your striving for what has already been guaranteed to you,
and your remissness in what is demanded of you,
are signs of the blurring of your intellect.[6]

6

If in spite of intense supplication,
there is delay in the timing of the Gift,[7]
let that not be the cause for your despairing.
For He has guaranteed you a response
in what He chooses for you,
not in what you choose for yourself,
and at the time He desires, not the time you desire.

7

If what was promised does not occur,
even though the time for its occurrence had been fixed,
then that must not make you doubt the promise.
Otherwise your intellect will be obscured
and the light of your innermost heart extinguished.[8]

8

If He opens a door for you, thereby making Himself known,
pay no heed if your deeds do not measure up to this.
For, in truth, He has not opened it for you
but out of a desire to make Himself known to you.
Do you not know that He is the one
who presented the knowledge of Himself to you,
whereas you are the one
who presented Him with deeds?
What a difference between
what He brings to you and what you present to Him![9]

9

Actions differ
because the inspirations of the states of being differ.[10]

10

Actions are lifeless forms,
but the presence of an inner reality of sincerity within them
is what endows them with life-giving Spirit.[11]

11

Bury your existence in the earth of obscurity,
for whatever sprouts forth,
without having first been buried,
flowers imperfectly. [12]

Unless the seed die...

12

Nothing benefits the heart more than a spiritual retreat
wherein it enters the domain
of meditation. [13]

13

How can the heart be illumined
while the forms of creatures are reflected in its mirror? [14]
Or how can it journey to God
while shackled by its passions?
Or how can it desire to enter the Presence of God
while it has not yet purified itself
of the stain of forgetfulness?
Or how can it understand the subtle points of mysteries
while it has not yet repented of its offenses?

14

The Cosmos is all darkness.
It is illumined only by the manifestation of God in it.
Whoever sees the Cosmos and does not contemplate Him
in it or by it or before it or after it is in need of light
and is veiled from the sun of gnosis
by the clouds of created things. [15]

15

That which shows you the existence of His Omnipotence
is that He veiled you from Himself
by what has no existence alongside of Him. [16]

16

How can it be conceived that something veils Him,
since He is the One who manifests everything?[17]
How can it be conceived that something veils Him,
since He is the one who is manifest *through* everything?
How can it be conceived that something veils Him,
since He is the One who is manifest *in* everything?
How can it be conceived that something veils Him,
since He is the Manifest *to* everything?
How can it be conceived that something veils Him,
since He was the Manifest *before* the existence of anything?
How can it be conceived that something veils Him,
since He is more manifest than anything?
How can it be conceived that something veils Him,
since He is the One alongside of whom there is nothing?[18]
How can it be conceived that something veils Him,
since He is nearer to you than anything else?[19]
How can it be conceived that something veils Him,
since, were it not for Him,
the existence of everything would not have been manifest?
It is a marvel how Being has been manifested in nonbeing,
and how the contingent has been established
alongside of Him who possesses the attribute of Eternity![20]

Chapter 2

And he said (may God be pleased with him!):

17

He who wishes that there appear, at a given moment,
other than what God has manifested in it,
has not left ignorance behind at all![21]

18

Your postponement of deeds till the time when you are free
is one of the frivolities of the ego.[22]

19

Do not request Him to get you out of a state
so as to make use of you in a different one;
for, were He to desire so, He could make use of you
as you are, without taking you out![23]

20

Hardly does the intention of the initiate
want to stop at what has been revealed to him,
than the voices of Reality call out to him:
"That which you are looking for is still ahead of you!"
And hardly do the exterior aspects of created beings
display their charms,
than their inner realities call out to him:
"We are only a trial, so disbelieve not!"[24]

21

Your requesting Him is suspecting Him.
Your seeking Him is due to your absence from Him.

Your seeking someone else
is because of your immodesty toward Him.
Your requesting
someone else
is on account of your distance from Him.[25]

22
Not a breath do you expire
but a Decree of Destiny makes it go forth.[26]

23
Do not look forward to being free of alterities,
for that is indeed what cuts you off from vigilant attention to
Him
in that very state He has assigned to you.[27]

24
So long as you are in this world,
be not surprised at the existence of sorrows.
For, truly, it manifests nothing but what is in keeping
with its character or its inevitable nature.[28]

25
No search pursued with the help of your Lord
remains at a standstill,
but any search pursued by yourself
will not be fruitful.

26
Among the signs of success at the end
is the turning to God at the beginning.

27
He who is illumined at the beginning
is illumined at the end.[29]

28

Whatever is deposited in the invisible world
of innermost hearts
is manifested in the visible world
of phenomena.[30]

29

What a difference between one who proceeds *from* God
in his argumentation
and one who proceeds inferentially *to* Him!
He who has Him as his starting-point knows the Real
as It is,
and proves any matter by reference to the Being of its
Origin.
But inferential argumentation
comes from the absence of union with Him.
Otherwise, when was it that he became absent
that one has to proceed inferentially to Him?
Or when was it that He became distant
that created things themselves will unite us to Him?[31]

30

Those who are united with Him:
"Let him who has abundance spend out of his abundance."[32]
Those who are voyaging toward Him:
"And whoever has his means of subsistence
straitened. . . ."[33]

31

Those who are voyaging to Him
are guided by the lights of their orientation,
whereas those who are united to Him
have the lights of face-to-face confrontation.
The former belong to their lights,
whereas the lights belong to the latter,
for they belong to God and to nothing apart from Him.
"Say: *Allah*! Then leave them prattling in their vain talk."[34]

Chapter 3

And he said (may God be pleased with him!):

32
Your being on the lookout for the vices
hidden within you
is better than
your being on the lookout for the invisible realities
veiled from you.[35]

33
The Real is not veiled from you.
Rather, it is you who are veiled from seeing It;
for, were anything to veil It,
then that which veils It would cover It.
But if there were a covering to It,
then that would be a limitation to Its Being:
Every limitation to anything has power over it.
"And He is the Omnipotent, above His servants."[36]

34
Among the attributes of your human nature,
draw away
from every one that is incompatible with your servanthood,
so that you may be responsive to the call of God
and near His Presence.

35

The source
of every disobedience, indifference, and passion
is self-satisfaction.
The source
of every obedience, vigilance, and virtue
is dissatisfaction with one's self.
It is better for you to keep company with an ignorant man
dissatisfied with himself
than to keep company with a learned man
satisfied with himself.
For what knowledge is there in a self-satisfied scholar?
And what ignorance is there in an unlearned man
dissatisfied with himself?

36

The ray of light of the intellect
makes you witness His nearness to you.
The eye of the intellect
makes you witness your nonbeing as due to His Being.
The Truth of the intellect
makes you witness His Being,
not your nonbeing, nor your being.[37]

37

"God was, and there was nothing with Him,
and He is now as He was."[38]

Chapter 4

And he said (may God be pleased with Him!):

38
Let not the intention of your aspiration shift
to what is other than He,
for one's hopes cannot outstrip the Generous.

39
Appeal to no one but Him to relieve you of a pressing need
that He Himself has brought upon you.
For how can someone else remove what He has imposed?
And how can he who is unable to free himself
of a pressing need
free someone else of one?

40
If you have not improved your thinking of Him
because of His ineffable nature,
improve it because of His treatment of you.
For has He accustomed you to anything but what is good?
And has He conferred upon you anything but His favors?

41
How astonishing is he who flees from what is inescapable
and searches for what is evanescent!
"For surely it is not the eyes that are blind,
but blind are the hearts which are in the breasts."[39]

42
Travel not from creature to creature,
otherwise you will be like a donkey at the mill:
Roundabout he turns, his goal the same as his departure.
Rather, go from creatures to the Creator:
"And that the final end is unto thy Lord."[40]
Consider the Prophet's words (God bless him and grant him
peace!):
"Therefore, he whose flight is for God and His Messenger,
then his flight is for God and His Messenger;
and he whose flight is for worldly gain
or marriage with a woman,
then his flight is for that which he flees to."
So understand his words (upon him peace!)
and ponder this matter, if you can.
And peace on you!

Chapter 5

And he said (God be pleased with him!):

43
Do not keep company
with anyone whose state does not inspire you
and whose speech does not lead you
to God.

44
You might be in a bad state; then,
associating with one who is in a worse state,
you see virtue in yourself.

45
No deed arising from a renouncing heart is small,
and no deed arising from an avaricious heart is fruitful.

46
Good works
are the results of good states.
Good states
arise from the stations wherein abide
those who have spiritual realization.

47
Do not abandon the Invocation
because you do not feel the Presence of God therein.
For your forgetfulness *of* the Invocation of Him

is worse than your forgetfulness *in* the Invocation of Him.
Perhaps He will take you from an Invocation with
forgetfulness
to one with vigilance, and from one with vigilance
to one with the Presence of God, and from one with the
Presence of God
to one wherein everything but the Invoked is absent.
"And that is not difficult for God."[41]

Chapter 6

And he said (may God be pleased with him!):

48
A sign of the heart's death
is the absence of sadness
over the acts of obedience you have neglected
and the abandonment of regret
over the mistakes you have made.

49
Let no sin reach such proportions in your eyes
that it cuts you off from having a good opinion of God,
for, indeed, whoever knows his Lord
considers his sin as paltry next to His generosity.

50
There is no minor sin when His justice confronts you;
and there is no major sin when His grace confronts you.

51
No deed is more fruitful for the heart
than the one you are not aware of
and which is deemed paltry by you.

52
He only made an inspiration come upon you
so that you would go to him.[42]

53

He made an inspiration come upon you
so as to get you out of the grip of alterities
and free you from bondage to created things.

54

He made an inspiration come upon you
so as to take you out of the prison of your existence
into the unlimited space of your contemplation.

55

Lights are the riding-mounts of hearts
and of their innermost centers.[43]

56

Light is the army of the heart,
just as darkness is the army of the soul.
So when God wishes to come to the help of His servant,
He furnishes him with armies of lights
and cuts off from him the reinforcements
of darkness and alterities.

57

Insight belongs to the Light,
discernment to the intellect,
and both progression and retrogression belong to the heart.[44]

58

Let not obedience make you joyous
because it comes from you;
but rather, be joyous over it
because it comes from God to you.
"Say: In the grace of God and in His mercy,
in that they should rejoice.
It is better than that which they hoard."[45]

59

He prevents those who are voyaging to Him
from witnessing their deeds
and those who are united with Him
from contemplating their states.
He does that for the voyagers because
they have not realized sincerity toward God in those works;
and He does that for those united with Him because
He makes them absent from contemplating those states
by contemplating Him.

Chapter 7

And he said (may God be pleased with him!):

60
Were it not for the sceds of ambitious desire,
the branches of disgrace would not be lofty.

61
Nothing leads you so much like suspicion.[46]

62
In your despairing, you are a free man;
but in your coveting, you are a slave.

63
Whoever does not draw near to God
as a result of the carcsses of love
is shackled to Him with the chains of misfortune.

64
Whoever is not thankful for graces
runs the risk of losing them;
and whoever is thankful,
fetters them with their own cords.

65
Be fearful lest the existence of His generosity toward you
and the persistence of your bad behavior toward Him
not lead you step by step to ruin.
"We shall lead them to ruin step by step
from whence they know not."[47]

66

It is ignorance on the part of the novice to act improperly,
and then, his punishment having been delayed,
to say, "If this had been improper conduct,
He would have shut off help and imposed exile."
Help could be withdrawn from him
without his being aware of it,
if only by blocking its increase.
And it could be that you are made to abide at a distance
without your knowing it,
if only by His leaving you to do as you like.

67

If you see a servant
whom God has made to abide in the recitation of litanies
and prolonged His help therein,
do not disdain what his Lord has given him
on the score that you do not detect the signs of gnostics on
him
nor the splendor of God's lovers.
For had there been no inspiration,
there would have been no litany.

68

God makes some people remain in the service of Him,
and He singles out others to love Him.
"All do we aid—these as well as those—
out of the bounty of thy Lord,
and the bounty of thy Lord is not limited."[48]

Chapter 8

And he said (may God be pleased with him!):

69
It is rare that divine inspirations come except suddenly,
and this, so that they be protected
from servants' claiming them
by virtue of the existence of receptivity on their part.

70
Infer the presence of ignorance
in anyone whom you see answering all that he is asked
or giving expression to all that he witnesses
or mentioning all that he knows.

71
He made the Hereafter an abode
to reward his believing servants
only because this world cannot contain
what He wishes to bestow upon them
and because He deemed their worth too high
to reward them in a world without permanence.

72
Whoever finds the fruit of his deeds coming quickly
has proof of the fact of acceptance.[49]

73
If you want to know your standing with Him,
look at the state He has put you in now.

74

When He gives you obedience,
making you unaware of it because of Him,
then know that He has showered you liberally with His
graces
both inwardly and outwardly.

Chapter 9

And he said (may God be pleased with him!):

75
The best that you can seek from Him
is that which He seeks from you.[50]

76
One of the signs of delusion
is sadness over the loss of obedience
coupled with an absence of resolve to bring it back to life.

77
The gnostic is not one who,
when making a symbolic allusion,
finds God nearer to himself than his symbolic allusion.
Rather, the gnostic is the one who,
because of his self-extinction in His Being
and self-absorption in contemplating Him,
has no symbolic allusion.[51]

78
Hope goes hand in hand with deeds;
otherwise, it is just wishful thinking.

79
That which the gnostics seek from God
is sincerity in servanthood
and performance of the rights of Lordship.

80

He expanded you so as not to keep you in contraction;
He contracted you so as not to keep you in expansion;
and He took you out of both
so that you not belong to anything apart from Him.[52]

81

It is more dreadful for gnostics
to be expanded than to be contracted,
for only a few
can stay within the limits of proper conduct in expansion.

82

Through the existence of joy
the soul gets its share in expansion,
but there is no share for the soul in contraction.

83

Sometimes He gives while depriving you,
and sometimes He deprives you in giving.

84

When he opens up your understanding of deprivation,
deprivation becomes the same as giving.

85

Outwardly, creatures are an illusion;
but, inwardly, they are an admonition.
Thus, the soul looks at the illusory exterior
while the heart looks at the admonitory interior.[53]

86

If you want a glory that does not vanish,
then do not glory in a glory that vanishes.

87
The real journey
is when the world's dimensions are rolled away from you
so that you see the Hereafter closer to you than yourself.[54]

88
A gift from man is deprivation;
but deprivation from God is beneficence.

Chapter 10

And he said (may God be pleased with him!):

89
Far be it from our Lord
to recompense with credit
the servant who deals with Him in cash![55]

90
Suffice it
as a recompense to you for obedience
that He has judged you worthy of obedience.

91
It suffices as a reward for the ones who do good
that He has inspired obedience to Him in their hearts
and brought upon them a state of reciprocal intimacy with
Him.

92
Whoever worships Him for something he hopes for from Him,
or in order to stave off the arrival of chastisement,
has not concerned himself
with the true nature of His Attributes.

93
When He gives, He shows you His kindness;
when He deprives, He shows you His power;
and in all that, He is making Himself known to you
and coming to you with His gentleness.

94

Deprivation hurts you
only because of your incomprehension of God in it.

95

Sometimes He opens the door of obedience for you,
but not the door of acceptance;
or sometimes He condemns you to sin,
and it turns out to be a cause for union with God.[56]

96

A disobedience that bequeathes humiliation and extreme need
is better than an obedience that bequeathes self-infatuation and
pride.

97

There are two graces that no being can do without
and that are necessary for every creature:
the grace of existence, and the grace of sustenance.

98

He bestowed His grace upon you,
first, through giving you existence,
and, second, through uninterrupted sustenance.

99

Your indigence belongs to you essentially,
for accidents do not abolish essential indigence:
The trials that arrive in this world
are but reminders to you of what you ignore of indigence.[57]

100

Your best moment
is the one wherein you witness your actual indigence
and, through it,
reach the reality of your lowliness.

101

When He alienates you from His creatures,
then know that He wants
to open for you the door of intimacy with Himself.

102

When He loosens your tongue with a request,
then know that He wants to give you something.

103

The imperative need of the gnostic never vanishes,
nor is his repose in anything but God.[58]

104

He illumined exterior phenomena
with the lights of His created things;
and He illumined the innermost hearts
with the uncreated lights of His attributes.
For that reason,
the lights of exterior phenomena set,
whereas the lights of hearts
—and of the innermost hearts—
do not set.
That is why it is said, "Verily, the sun of the day sets at night,
but the Sun of hearts never sets!"[59]

Chapter 11

And he said (may God be pleased with him!):

105
To soften for you the suffering of affliction,
He has taught you
that He is the one who causes trials to come upon you.
For the one who confronts you with His Decrees of Fate
is the same one who has accustomed you to His good choice.

106
Whoever supposes that His gentleness
is separate from His Decree of Fate
does so out of shortsightedness.

107
It is not feared
that the ways leading to God be confusing to you;
but rather, it is feared
that passion overcome you.[60]

108
Praise be to Him
who has hidden the inner reality of holiness
by manifesting the quality of human nature,
and who has appeared in the sublimity of Lordship
by manifesting the attribute of servanthood.[61]

109

Do not press claims against your Lord
because your request has been delayed;
instead, press claims against yourself
for slackening in your behavior.

110

When He makes you submissive to His command outwardly
and provides you with resignation to His power inwardly,
then He has truly enhanced the favor accorded you.

111

Not all who are most certainly among the chosen
go on to perfect their liberation.[62]

Chapter 12

And he said (may God be pleased with him!):

112
Only the ignorant man scorns the recitation of litany.
Inspiration is to be found in the Hereafter,
while the litany vanishes with the vanishing of this world;
but it is more fitting to be occupied with something
for which there is no substitute.
The litany is what He seeks from you;
the inspiration is what you seek from Him.
What comparison is there
between what He seeks from you and what you seek from
Him?[63]

113
The arrival of sustenance
is in accordance with receptivity,
while the raying-out of lights
is in accordance with the purity of the innermost being.[64]

114
When the forgetful man gets up in the morning,
he reflects on what he is going to do,
whereas the intelligent man *sees* what God is doing with him.

115
The devotees and the ascetics are alienated from everything
only because of their absence from God in everything.
Had they contemplated Him in everything,
they would not have been alienated from anything.[65]

116

He commanded you in this world
to reflect upon His creations;
but in the Hereafter
He will reveal to you the perfection of His Essence.

117

When He knew that you would not renounce Him,
He made you contemplate that which issues *from* Him.[66]

118

Since God knows of the occurrence of weariness on your
part,
He has varied the acts of obedience for you;
and since He knows of the occurrence of impulsiveness in
you,
He has limited them to specific times,
so that your concern be with the performance of ritual
prayer,
not with the existence of the ritual prayer.
Not everyone who prays performs well.[67]

119

Ritual prayer is a purification for hearts
and an opening-up of the door of the invisible domains.

120

Ritual prayer is the place of intimate conversations
and a mine of reciprocal acts of purity
wherein the regions of the innermost being are expanded
and the rising gleams of light shine forth.
He knew of the existence of weakness in you,
so He made the number of ritual prayers small;
and He knew of your need of His grace,
so He multiplied their fruitful results.

121

When you seek a recompense for a deed,
the reality of sincerity in it is demanded of you in return.
As for the insincere,
the feeling of security from chastisement suffices him.

122

Do not seek recompense for a deed whose doer was not you.
It suffices you as recompense for the deed that He accepts it.[68]

123

When He wants to show His grace to you,
He creates states in you and attributes them to you.[69]

124

Were He to make you go back to yourself,
there would be no end to the reasons for blaming you;
and were He to manifest His beneficence toward you,
there would be no end to the reasons for praising you.

Chapter 13

And he said (may God be pleased with him!):

125
Cling to the attributes of His Lordship
and realize the attributes of your servanthood!

126
He has prohibited you from claiming for yourself,
among the qualities of created beings,
that which does not belong to you;
so would He permit you to lay claim to His Attribute,
He who is the Lord of the Universe?

127
How can the laws of nature be ruptured for you
so that miracles result,
while you, for your part,
have yet to rupture your bad habits?[70]

128
The point at issue
is not the fact of searching;
rather, the point at issue
is that you be provisioned with virtuous conduct.

129
Nothing pleads on your behalf like extreme need,
nor does anything speed gifts to you quicker
than lowliness and want.

130

If you were to be united with Him
only after the extinction of your vices
and the effacement of your pretensions,
you would never be united with Him!
Instead, when He wants to unite you to Himself,
He covers your attribute with His Attribute
and hides your quality with His Quality.
And thus He unites you to Himself
by virtue of what comes from Him to you,
not by virtue of what goes from you to Him.[71]

Chapter 14

And he said (may God be pleased with him!):

131
Were it not for the kindliness of His veiling,
no deed would be worthy of acceptance.[72]

132
You are more in need of His forbearance when you obey
Him
than you are when you disobey Him.[73]

133
Veiling is of two kinds:
veiling *of* disobedience, and veiling *in* it.
Common people seek God's veiling
in disobedience
out of the fear of falling in rank among mankind.
The elect seek the veiling of disobedience
out of the fear of falling from the sight of God,
the True King.

134
Whoever honors you honors only the beauty of His veil in
you.
Therefore, praise is to Him who veiled you,
not to the one who honored and thanked you.[74]

135
No one is a friend of yours
except the one who, while knowing your defects, is your

companion,
and that is only your generous Master.
The best one to have as a friend
is He who does not seek you out
for the sake of something coming from you to Him.

136

Were the light of certitude to shine,
you would see the Hereafter so near
that you could not move toward it,
and you would see that the eclipse of extinction
had come over the beauties of the world.

137

It is not the existence of any being alongside of Him
that veils you from God,
for nothing is alongside of Him.
Rather, what veils you from Him
is the illusion of a being alongside of Him.[75]

138

Had it not been for His manifestation in created beings,
eyesight would not have perceived them.
Had His Qualities been manifested,
His created beings would have disappeared.[76]

139

He manifests everything
because He is the Interior,
and He conceals the existence of everything
because He is the Exterior.[77]

140

He has permitted you to reflect
on what is *in* created beings,
but He has not allowed you to stop at the selfsame creatures.

"Say: Behold what is in the heavens and the earth!"[78]
Thus, with His words "Behold what is in the heavens"
He opened up the door of instruction for you.
But He did not say, "Behold the heavens,"
so as not to lead you to the mere existence of bodies.

141
The Universe is permanent through His making it permanent,
and it is annihilated by the Unity of His Essence.[79]

Chapter 15

And he said (may God be pleased with him!):

142
People praise you for what they suppose is in you;
but you must blame your soul for what you know is in it.

143
When the believer is praised,
he is ashamed before God that he should be lauded
for an attribute he does not see in himself.

144
The most ignorant of all people
is the one who abandons the certitude he has for an opinion
people have.

145
When He lets praise of you burst forth,
and you are not worthy of it,
praise Him for what He is worthy of.

146
When ascetics are praised, they are contracted,
for they witness the praise as coming from mankind;
but when gnostics are praised, they are expanded,
for they witness the praise as coming from the True King.

147

If when given something, the giving expands you,
and if when deprived of something, the deprivation contracts
you,
then take that as proof of your immaturity
and the insincerity of your servanthood.

Chapter 16

And he said (may God be pleased with him!):

148
When you commit a sin,
let that not be a reason for despairing
of attaining to righteousness before your Lord,
for that might be the last one decreed for you.

149
If you want the door of hope opened for you,
then consider what comes to you from Him;
but if you want the door of sadness opened for you,
then consider what goes to Him from you.

150
Sometimes He makes you learn in the night of contraction
what you have not learned in the radiance of the day of
expansion.
"You do not know which of them is nearer to you in
benefit."[80]

151
The hearts and the innermost centers of being
are the places where lights arise.[81]

152
There is a light deposited in hearts
that is nourished by the Light
coming from the treasuries of the invisible realms.

153

There is a light
wherewith He unveils for you His created things,
and there is a Light
wherewith He unveils for you His Attributes. [82]

154

Sometimes hearts stop at lights
the same way souls are veiled
by the opacities of alterities.

155

By way of honoring them,
He veiled the lights of the innermost hearts
with the opacities of exterior phenomena
so that they would not be abused when expressing
themselves
nor be accused of seeking renown. [83]

Chapter 17

And he said (may God be pleased with him!):

156
Glory be to Him
who has not made any sign leading to His saints
save as a sign leading to Himself,
and who has joined no one to them
except him whom God wants to join to Himself. [84]

157
Sometimes He reveals to you
the invisible domain of His Realm
but veils you
from knowing the secrets of servants.

158
Whoever gets to know the secrets of servants
without patterning himself on the divine mercifulness
finds his knowledge a tribulation
and a cause for drawing evil upon himself.

159
The ego's share in disobedience is outwardly clear,
while its share in obedience is inwardly hidden.
To cure what is hidden is hard indeed!

160
Sometimes ostentation penetrates you in such a way
that no one notices it.

161

Your desire that people know your particular distinction
is a proof of insincerity in your servanthood. [85]

162

Make mankind's looking at you disappear
by being content with God's looking at you!
Slip away from their approach to you
by contemplating His approach to you!

163

He who knows God contemplates Him in everything.
He who is extinguished by Him is absent from everything.
He who loves Him prefers nothing to Him.

164

Only His extreme nearness to you
is what veils God from you. [86]

165

Only because of the intensity of His manifestation
is He veiled,
and only because of the sublimity of His Light
is He hidden from view.

Chapter 18

And he said (may God be pleased with him!):

166
Let not your asking be the cause of His giving,
for then your understanding of Him might diminish.
Let your asking be for the sake of showing servanthood
and fulfilling the rights of Lordship.

167
How can your subsequent asking
be the cause of His prior giving?[87]

168
Far be it from the Decree of the Eternal
to subject to contingent causes.[88]

169
His providential care of you
is not due to anything coming from you.
Where were you when He confronted you with His
providence
or met you face-to-face with His care?
Neither sincerity of deeds nor the existence of states
has any being in His Eternity.
Instead, only pure bestowing and sublime giving are there.[89]

170
He knew that servants would anticipate
the emergence of the mystery of providence in themselves,

so He said, "He chooses whom He pleases for His
Mercy."[90]
And He knew that, had He left them at that,
they would have abandoned all effort by relying on the
Eternal,
so He said,
"Surely the Mercy of God is night to the doers of good."[91]

171
Everything depends on the Divine Will,
but It Itself depends on nothing at all.[92]

Chapter 19

And he said (may God be pleased with him!):

172
Sometimes virtuous behavior
leads some to abandon asking
because of trust in His Providence
or because concern for the Invocation of Him
stymies their asking of Him.[93]

173
Only he to whom forgetfulness is possible
is to be reminded;
and only he to whom inattention is possible
is to be warned.

174
The feast days of novices are when states of need arrive.[94]

175
Sometimes you will find more benefit in states of need
than you will find in fasting or ritual prayer.

176
States of need are gift-laden carpets.

177
If you want gifts to come your way,
then perfect the spiritual poverty you have.
"Alms are only for the poor."[95]

178
Realize your attributes
and He will help you with His Attributes;
realize your lowliness
and He will help you with His Sublimity;
realize your impotence
and He will help you with His Power;
realize your weakness
and He will help you with His Might and Force![96]

Chapter 20

And he said (may God be pleased with him!):

179
Sometimes a charisma is bestowed
upon someone whose righteousness is not perfect.[97]

180
A sign that it is God who has put you in a certain state
is that He keeps you in it while its fruits mature.[98]

181
He who holds forth
from the standpoint of his own virtuous behavior
will be silenced by misbehavior toward God;
but he who holds forth
from the standpoint of God's virtuous behavior toward him
will not be silenced when he misbehaves.[99]

182
The lights of sages precede their words,
so that, wherever illumination occurs, there the expression
arrives.

183
Every utterance that issues forth
does so with the vestment of the heart from which it
emerged.[100]

184
Whoever has been given permission to speak out
will find that his expression is understood by his listeners
and that his symbolic allusion is clear to them.

185
Sometimes the lights of inner realities will appear eclipsed
when you have not been given permission to express them.

186
Their expression
is either because of the overflow of ecstasy
or for the purpose of guiding a disciple.
The former case is that of those who are voyaging;
the latter case is that of those who possess a function
and have realization.[101]

187
An expression is nourishment to needy listeners,
and your share in it is only what you can eat thereof.

188
Sometimes he who draws near to a station
expresses himself about it,
and sometimes he who is united with it
expresses himself about it.
That is confusing save to him who has insight.[102]

189
He who is voyaging should not express his inspirations,
for that indeed diminishes their activity in his heart
and strips him of sincerity with his Lord.[103]

190

Do not stretch out your hand to take from creatures
unless you see that the Giver among them is your Lord.
If such is the case,
then take what knowledge says is suitable for you.[104]

191

Sometimes the gnostic is ashamed
of submitting his urgent need to his Lord,
being content with His Will.
So why should he not be ashamed
of submitting his urgent need to a creature of His?[105]

Chapter 21

And he said (may God be pleased with him!):

192
When two matters seem confusing to you,
see which is heavier on the ego and follow it through.
For, truly, nothing weighs on the ego but that which is true.

193
A sign of compliance with passion
is haste in supererogatory deeds
and sluggishness in fulfilling obligatory deeds.[106]

194
He laid down specific times for acts of obedience
so that procrastination not divert you from them,
and He made each time span ample
so that you would have a share in making the choice.[107]

195
He knew of the irresolution of servants in dealing with Him,
so He made obedience to Him obligatory for them.
He drove them to obedience with the chains of obligation.
"Your Lord is amazed at people
who are driven to Paradise with chains!"[108]

196
He made the service of Him
obligatory upon you,

which is as much as to say that He made entry into His
Paradise
obligatory for you.

197
Whoever finds it astonishing
that God should save him from his passion
or yank him out of his forgetfulness
has deemed the divine Power to be weak.
"And God has power over everything."[109]

198
Sometimes darknesses come over you
in order that He make you aware
of the value of His blessings upon you.

199
He who does not know the value of graces
when they are present
knows their value
when they are absent.

200
The inspirations of grace should not so dazzle you
as to keep you from fulfilling the obligations of thankfulness,
for that would indeed bring you down in rank.[110]

201
Incurable sickness results when the sweetness of passion
takes possession of the heart.

202
Only an unsettling fear or a restless desire
can expell passion from the heart.[111]

203
Just as He does not love the deed
possessed of associationism,
so similarly He does not love the heart
possessed of associationism.
As for the deed possessed of associationism,
He does not accept it;
and as for the heart possessed of associationism,
He does not draw near to it.[112]

Chapter 22

And he said (may God be pleased with him!):

204
There are lights that are allowed to arrive
and lights that are allowed to enter.[113]

205
Sometimes lights come upon you
and find the heart stuffed with the forms of created things;
so they go back from whence they descended.[114]

206
Empty your heart of altcritics
and you will fill it up with gnostic intuitions and mysteries.

207
Do not deem His giving to be slow;
but rather, deem your approaching to be slow.

208
It is possible to fulfill some obligations at times,
but it is impossible to fulfill the obligations of every
moment,
for there is no moment wherein God does not hold against
you
a new obligation or a definite matter.
So how can you fulfill therein someone else's obligation
when you have not fulfilled God's?

209
That part of your life that has gone by
is irreplaceable,
and that which has arrived
is priceless.

210
You have not loved anything without being its slave,
but He does not want you to be someone else's slave.

211
Your obedience does not benefit Him,
and your disobedience does not harm Him.
It is only for your own good
that He commanded the one and prohibited the other.

212
His Sublimity is not increased
when someone draws near to Him,
and His Sublimity is not decreased
when someone draws away from Him.

Chapter 23

And he said (may God be pleased with him!):

213

Your union with God is union through knowledge of Him.
Otherwise, God is beyond being united with anything
or anything being united with Him![115]

214

Your nearness to Him is that you contemplate His nearness.
Otherwise, what comparison is there between you and His
nearness?

215

Inner realities arrive synthetically
in the state of illumination,
and after retention comes their explanation.
"So when We recite it, follow its recitation.
Again on us rests the explaining of it."[116]

216

When divine inspirations come upon you,
they demolish your habits.
"Surely the kings, when they enter a town, ruin it."[117]

217

Inspiration comes from the Presence of the Omnipotent.
As a result, nothing opposes it without being smashed to
bits.
"Nay, but We hurl the Truth against falsehood,
and It prevails against it, and lo! falsehood vanishes."[118]

218

How can God be veiled by anything,
for He is apparent
and has actual being in that wherewith He is veiled?[119]

219

Do not lose hope
in the acceptance of an act of yours
wherein you found no awareness of the divine Presence.
Sometimes He accepts an act
the fruit of which you have not perceived right away.

220

Attest not to the validity of an inspiration
whose fruits you know not.
The purpose of rainclouds is not to give rain;
their purpose is only to bring forth fruit.[120]

221

After the lights of inspirations have radiated forth
and their mysteries been deposited,
seek not their continuance,
for you have in God one who enables you to dispense with
everything,
but nothing enables you to dispense with God.

222

The proof that you have not found Him
is that you strive for the permanency of what is
other-than-He;
and the proof that you are not united to Him
is that you feel estranged at the loss of what is
other-than-He.[121]

Chapter 24

And he said (may God be pleased with him!):

223
While varied in its manifestations,
felicity is only for the sake of contemplating and drawing
near to Him;
and, while varied in its manifestations,
suffering is due only to the existence of His veil.
Therefore, the existence of the veil is the cause of suffering,
and the perfection of felicity
is through the vision of the Countenance of God, the
Generous.[122]

224
That which hearts find in the way of worries and sadnesses
is due to that which prevents them from having inner
vision.[123]

225
Part of the completeness of grace accorded you
lies in His providing you with what suffices
and holding you back from what makes you exceed bounds.

226
In order that your sadness over anything be little,
let your joy over it be little.

227
If you do not want to be dismissed,
then do not take over a post that will not always be yours.[124]

228

If beginnings make you desirous,
endings will make you abstinent:
if their exteriors invited you,
their interiors will hold you back.[125]

229

He only made the world
the place of alterities and the mine of impurities
by way of inducing detachment toward it in you.

230

He knew you would not accept mere counsel,
so He made you sample the world's taste to a degree
that separation from it would be easy for you.

231

Beneficial knowledge
is the one whose ray of light expands in the mind
and uncovers the veil over the heart.[126]

232

The best knowledge is the one accompanied by fear.[127]

233

If fear is united with knowledge, then it is for you;
if not, then it is against you.

234

When it pains you that people do not come to you,
or that they do so with rebukes,
then return to the knowledge of God in you.
But if the knowledge of Him in you does not satisfy you,
then your affliction at *not* being content with that knowledge
is greater than your affliction at the pain coming from
people.

235

He only made affliction come at the hands of people
so that you not repose in them.
He wants to drive you out of everything
so that nothing would divert you from Him.

236

If you know that the devil does not forget you,
then do not, for your part,
forget Him who has your forelock in His hand.

237

He made the devil your enemy
so that, through him, He could drive you toward Himself,
and He stirred up your soul against you ·
so that your drawing near to Him would be permanent.

Chapter 25

And he said (may God be pleased with him!):

238
He who attributes humility to himself is really proud,
for humility arises only out of a loftiness;
so, when you attribute humility to yourself, then you are
proud.[128]

239
The humble man is not the one
who, when humble, sees that he is above what he does;
instead, the humble man is the one
who, when humble, sees that he is below what he does.[129]

240
Real humility is the one that arises
from the contemplation of His Sublimity
and the illumination of His Attribute.[130]

241
Only the contemplation of His Attribute
can dislodge you from your attribute.

242
The believer
is he who is diverted from extolling himself
by the praise of God,
and who is diverted from remembering his good fortune
by the fulfillment of God's rights.[131]

243
The lover is not the one
who hopes for a recompense from his beloved
or seeks some object.
In truth, the lover is the one
who spends generously on you,
not the one on whom you spend generously.

244
Were it not for the arenas of the soul,
the voyaging of the adepts could not be realized:
There is no distance between you and Him
that could be traversed by your journey,
nor is there any particle between you and Him
that could be effaced by your union with Him.[132]

245
He put you in the intermediary world
between His Kingdom and His Realm
to teach you the majesty of your rank
among His created beings
and that you are a jewel
wherein the pearls of His creations are hidden.[133]

246
The Cosmos envelops you
in respect to your corporeal nature,
but it does not do so
in respect to the immutability of your spiritual nature.
So long as the domains of the Invisible Worlds
have not been revealed to him,
the creature in the Cosmos is imprisoned by his
surroundings
and confined in the temple of his nature.[134]

247

So long as you have not contemplated the Creator,
you belong to created beings;
but when you have contemplated Him,
created beings belong to you.

248

The permanence of sanctity does not necessitate
that the attribute of human nature be nonexistent.
Sanctity is analogous to the illumination of the sun in
daytime:
It appears on the horizon but it is not a part of it.
Sometimes the suns of His Attributes shine
in the night of your existence,
and sometimes He takes that away from you
and returns you to your existence.
So daytime is not from you to you,
but instead, it comes upon you.[135]

249

By the existence of His created things,
He points to the existence of His Names,
and by the existence of His Names,
He points to the existence of His Qualities,
and by the existence of His Qualities,
He points to the reality of His Essence,
for it is impossible for a quality to be self-subsistent.
He reveals the perfection of His Essence
to those who have attraction;
then He turns them back
to the contemplation of His Qualities;
then He turns them back
to dependence on His Names;
and then He turns them back
to the contemplation of His created things.

The contrary is the case for those who are initiates:
The end for those progressing
is the beginning for the ecstatics,
and the beginning for those progressing
is the end for the ecstatics.
But this is not to be taken literally,
since both might meet in the Path,
one in his descending, the other in his ascending.[136]

250

It is only in the invisible world of the Realm
that the value of the lights of hearts
and innermost centers of being is known,
just as the lights of the sky do not manifest themselves
except in the visible world of the Kingdom.[137]

251

For those who do good,
finding the fruits of the acts of obedience in this world
is glad tidings of their reward in the Hereafter.[138]

252

How can you seek recompense
for a deed He bestowed upon you out of charity?
Or how can you seek recompense
for a sincerity He gave you as a gift?

253

The lights of some people precede their invocations,
while the invocations of some people precede their lights.
There is the invoker who invokes so that his heart be
illumined;
and there is the invoker whose heart has been illumined—
and he invokes.[139]

254

The exterior of invocation would not exist
were it not for the interior of contemplation and
meditation.[140]

255

He made you witness before He asked you to give witness:
Thus, the outer faculties speak of His Divinity
while the heart and the innermost consciousness
have realized His Unity.

256

He ennobled you with three charismatic gifts:
He made you an invoker of Him,
and had it not been for His grace,
you would not have been worthy of the flow
of the invocation of Him in you;
He made you remembered by Him
inasmuch as He confirmed His relationship to you;
and He made you remembered by those with Him,
thereby perfecting His grace upon you.[141]

257

Many a life is long in years but meager in fruits,
and many a life is short in years but rich in fruits.

258

He who has been blessed in life
attains, in a short time, to such gifts from God
that no expression or symbolic allusion could describe.

259

It would be disappointing —really disappointing!—
if you were to find yourself free of distractions
and then not make toward Him,

or if you were to have few obstacles
and then not move on to Him!

260
Meditation is the voyage of the heart
in the domains of alterities.

261
Meditation is the lamp of the heart;
so when it goes away, the heart has no illumination.

262
Meditation is of two kinds:
the meditation of belief and faith,
and the meditation of contemplation and vision.
The first is for the adepts of reflective thought,
the second is for the adepts of contemplation
and intellectual vision.[142]

The First Treatise

Among the things he wrote to some of his friends, he said (may God be pleased with him!):

Now then, beginnings are the places where endings are revealed, so that whoever begins with God ends up with Him. He is the one you love and rush to in whatever occupies you, and He is the one you prefer in whatever you turn away from. Whoever is certain that God seeks him is sincere in seeking Him. He who knows that all matters are in God's hands is recollected through trust in Him. Truly, it is inevitable that the pillars of this world's house of existence be destroyed and its precious things be stripped away. For the intelligent man is more joyous over the permanent than he is over the evanescent. His lights shine forth, glad tidings have come to him. Thus, he turns away from this world, takes no notice of it, shuns it altogether. He does not therefore take it as a homeland, nor does he turn it into a home, but rather, while in it, he arouses his fervor toward God and seeks His help in going toward Him. His determination, a riding-mount, is restless and ever on the move till it comes to kneel down in the Presence of the Holy on the carpet of intimacy, the place of reciprocal disclosure, confrontation, companionship, conversation, contemplation, and looking.

The Presence is the nesting place of the hearts of initiates: They take refuge in it and dwell therein. Then, when they descend to the heaven of obligations and the earth of varied fortune, they do so with authority, stability, and profundity of certitude. For they have not descended to obligations through improper conduct or forgetfulness, nor to fortune through passion and pleasure; but instead they have entered therein by God and for God and from God and to God.

"And say: My Lord, make me enter a truthful entering, and make me go forth a truthful going forth,"[143] so that I will see Your strength and power when You make me enter, and will submit and conform myself to You when You make me go out. Give me an authority from You, an ally that helps me or that helps others through me, but not one that goes against me: one that helps me against self-regard and extinguishes me from the realm of my senses.

The Second Treatise

Among the things that he wrote to some of his friends, he said (may God be pleased with him!):

If the eye of the heart sees that God is One in His blessings, the Law requires nevertheless that thanks be given to His creatures.

Indeed, in the matter of blessings, people fall into three classes. The first is that of the forgetful person, immersed in his forgetfulness, strong in the domain of his senses, blurred in inner vision. He sees generosity as coming from mankind and does not contemplate it as coming from the Lord of the Universe, either out of conviction, in which case his associationism is evident, or else out of dependence, in which case his associationism is hidden.[144]

The second is that of the possessor of a spiritual reality who, by contemplating the True King, is absent from mankind, and who, by contemplating the Cause of effects, is extinguished from the effects. He is a servant brought face to face with Reality, the splendor of which is apparent in him. A traveler in the Path, he has mastered its extent, except that he is drowned in lights and does not perceive created things. His inebriety prevails over his sobriety, his union over his separation, his extinction over his permanence, and his absence over his presence.

The third is that of a servant who is more perfect than the second: He drinks, and increases in sobriety; he is absent, and increases in presence; his union does not veil him from his separation, nor does his separation veil him from his union; his extinction does not divert him from his permanence, nor does his permanence divert him fom his extinction. He acts justly toward everyone and gives everyone his proper due.[145]

Abu Bakr as-Siddiq said to A'isha, when her innocence was revealed through the tongue of the Prophet,[146] "O A'isha, be grateful to the Messenger of God!" Then she said, "By God, I will be grateful only to God!" Abu Bakr had pointed out to her the more perfect station, the station of permanence that requires the recognition of created things. God says, "Give thanks to Me and to thy parents."[147] And the Prophet said, "He who does not thank mankind does not thank God." At that time she was extinguished from her external senses, absent from created things, so that she contemplated the One, the Omnipotent.

The Third Treatise

He said (may God be pleased with him!):

When he was asked with regard to the Prophet's words, "And my eye's refreshment has been made to be in ritual prayer," whether that was particular to the Prophet or whether anyone else had a share or part in it, he answered:[148]

In truth, the eye's refreshment through contemplation is commensurate with the gnosis of the Object of contemplation. The gnosis of the Messenger is not like the gnosis of someone else; accordingly, someone else's refreshment of eye is not like his.

We have said that the refreshment of his eye in his ritual prayer was through his contemplating the Majesty of the Object of contemplation only because he himself indicated as much by his words, "in ritual prayer." For he did not say, "by means of ritual prayer," since his eye was not refreshed by means of something other than his Lord. How could it be otherwise? For he points to this station, and commands others to realize it, with his words, "Adore God as if you were seeing Him," since it would have been impossible for him to see Him and at the same time to witness someone other than He alongside of Him.

Suppose someone were to say, "The refreshment of the eye can be by means of ritual prayer because it is a grace of God and emerges from God's blessing itself. So, how is it one cannot ascend by means of it, or how is it the eye's refreshment cannot be had by means of it? For God says, 'Say: In the grace of God and in His mercy, in that they should rejoice.' "[149]

If that were said, then you must know that the significance of the verse, for those who meditate on the secret of the statement, is to be found in the main clause, for He says, "in that they should rejoice," and not, "in that you should rejoice, O Muhammad." In other words, "Say to them: Let them rejoice by means of generous acts and kindness, but let *your* rejoicing be with Him who is kind," just as, in another verse, He says, "Say: *Allah!* Then leave them prattling in their vain talk."[150]

The Fourth Treatise

Among the things he wrote to some of his friends, he said (may God be pleased with him!):

With regard to the advent of blessings, people are of three categories. To the first belongs the one who rejoices at blessings, not in respect to their Bestower or Originator, but in respect to his pleasure in them. This man belongs to the forgetful, and God's words hold true for him: "Until, when they rejoiced in what they were given, We seized them suddenly."[151]

To the second category belongs the one who rejoices at blessings inasmuch as he sees them as blessings from Him who sent them or as grace from Him who brought it to him. God refers to him with His words: "Say: In the grace of God and in His mercy, in that they should rejoice. It is better than that which they hoard."[152]

To the third category belongs the one who rejoices in God. Neither the exterior pleasure of blessings nor their interior graces divert him. Instead, his vision of God, his concentration on Him, divert him from what is other-than-He, so that he contemplates only Him. God refers to him with his words: "Say: *Allah!* Then leave them prattling in their vain talk."[153] God revealed to David: "O David, say to the truthful: Let them rejoice in Me, let them find joy in My invocation!"[154]

May God make your joy and ours in Him and in the contentment that comes from Him; may He put us among those who understand Him; may He not put us among the forgetful; and may He voyage with us in the path of the God-fearing with His grace and generosity!

Intimate Discourses

And he said (may God be pleased with him!):

1
My God,
I am poor in my richness,
so why should I not be poor in my poverty?[155]

2
My God,
I am ignorant in my knowledge,
so why should I not be most ignorant in my ignorance?

3
My God,
the diversity of Your planning
and the speed of Your predestined Decrees
prevent Your servants, the gnostics,
from relying on gifts or despairing of You during trials.[156]

4
My God,
from me comes what is in keeping with my miserliness,
and from You comes what is in keeping with Your
generosity.

5
My God,
You have attributed to Yourself
gentleness and kindness toward me

before the existence of my weakness;
so, would You then hold them back from me
after the existence of my weakness?[157]

6
My God,
if virtues arise from me,
that is because of Your grace:
It is Your right to bless me.
And if vices arise from me,
that is because of Your justice:
It is Your right to have proof against me.

7
My God,
how can You leave me to myself,
for You are responsible for me?
And how could I be harmed while You are my Ally?
Or how could I be disappointed in You, my Welcomer?
Here I am seeking to gain access to You
by means of my need of You.
How could I seek to gain access to You
by means of what cannot possibly reach you?
Or how can I complain to You of my state,
for it is not hidden from You?
Or how can I express myself to You in *my* speech,
since it comes from You and goes forth to You?
Or how can my hopes be dashed,
for they have already reached You?
Or how can my states not be good,
for they are based on You and go to You?

8 √
My God,
how gentle You are with me

in spite of my great ignorance,
and how merciful You are with me
in spite of my ugly deeds!

9

My God,
how near You are to me,
and how far I am from You!

10

My God,
how kind You are to me!
So what is it that veils me from You?

11

My God,
from the diversity of created things
and the changes of states,
I know that it is Your desire
to make Yourself known to me in everything
so that I will not ignore You in anything.

12

My God,
whenever my miserliness makes me dumb,
Your generosity makes me articulate,
and whenever my attributes make me despair,
Your grace gives me hope.

13

My God,
if someone's virtues are vices,
then why cannot his vices be vices?
And if someone's inner realities are pretensions,
then why cannot his pretensions be pretensions?[158]

14
My God,
Your penetrating decision and Your conquering will
have left no speech to the articulate
nor any state to him who has one!

15
My God, how often has Your justice destroyed
the dependence I built upon obedience
or the state I erected!
Yet, it was Your grace that freed me of them.

16
My God,
You know that,
even though obedience has not remained a resolute action
on my part,
it has remained as a love and a firm aspiration.

17
My God,
how can I resolve
while You are the Omnipotent,
or how can I *not* resolve
while you are the Commander?

18
My God,
my wavering among created things
inevitably makes the Sanctuary distant,
so unite me to You by means of a service that leads me to
You.

19
My God,
how can one argue inferentially of You

by that which depends on You for its existence?
Does anything other than You manifest what You do *not*
have,
so that it becomes the manifester *for* You?
When did You become so absent that You are in need of a
proof giving evidence of You?
And when did You become so distant
that it is created things themselves that lead us to You?[159]

20
My God,
blind is the eye
that does not see You watching over it,
and vain is the handclasp of a servant
who has not been given a share of Your love.

21 ✓
My God,
You have commanded me to return to created things,
so return me to them with the raiment of lights
and the guidance of inner vision,
so that I may return from them to You
just as I entered You from them,
with my innermost being protected from looking at them
and my fervor raised above dependence on them.
"Truly, over everything You are the Omnipotent."[160]

And he said (may God be pleased with him!):

22
My God,
here is my lowliness manifest before You,
and here is my state unhidden from You.
I seek from You union with You.
I proceed from You in my argumentation about You.

So guide me to You with Your light
and set me up before You through sincerity of servanthood!

23
My God,
make me know by means of Your treasured-up Knowledge,
and protect me by means of the mystery
of Your well-guarded Name.[161]!

24
My God,
make me realize the inner realities
of those drawn nigh,
and make me voyage in the path
of those possessed by attraction.[162]

25
My God,
through Your direction
make me dispense with self-direction,
and through Your choosing for me
make me dispense with my choosing;
and make me stand in the very center of my extreme need.

√ *26*
My God,
pull me out of my self-abasement
and purify me of doubting and associationism
before I descend into my grave.
I seek Your help, so help me.
In You I trust, so entrust me to no one else.
You do I ask, so do not disappoint me.
Your kindness do I desire, so do not refuse me.
It is to You that I belong, so do not banish me.
And it is at Your door that I stand, so do not cast me away.

27

My God,
Your Contentment is too holy
for there to be a cause for it in You,
so how can there be a cause for it in me?
Through Your Essence,
You are independent of any benefit coming to You,
so why should You not be independent of me?[163]

28 ✓

My God,
destiny and the Decree of Fate have overcome me,
and desire with its passional attachments
has taken me prisoner.
Be my Ally so that You may help me and others through
me.
Enrich me with Your kindness,
so that, content with You,
I can do without asking for anything.
You are the one who makes the lights shine in the hearts of
Your saints
so that they know You and affirm Your Oneness.
You are the one who makes alterities disappear
from the hearts of Your lovers
so that they love none but You and take refuge in none but
You.
You are the one who befriends them
when the world makes them forlorn.
You are the one who guides them
till the landmarks become clear for them.
He who has lost You—what has he found?
He who has found You—what has he lost?
Whoever takes someone other than You as a substitute
is disappointed,

and whoever wants to stray away from You
is lost.

29
My God,
how could hope be placed in what is other than You,
for You have not cut off Your benevolence?
And how could someone other than You be asked,
for You have not changed the norms for conferring
blessings?
O He who makes His beloved friends taste
the sweetness of intimacy with Himself
so that they stand before Him with praise,
and O He who clothes His saints
with the vestments of reverential fear toward Himself
so that they stand glorifying His glory—
You are the Invoker prior to invokers,
You are the Origin of benevolence prior to servants turning
to You,
You are the Munificent in giving prior to the asking of
seekers,
and You are the Giver who,
in respect to what You have given us,
asks us for a loan!

30
My God,
seek me with Your grace
so that I may reach You,
and attract me with Your blessings
so that I may draw near to You.

31
My God,
my hope is not cut off from You

even though I disobey You,
just as my fear does not leave me
even though I obey You.

32
My God,
the world has pushed me toward You,
and my knowledge of Your generosity has made me stand
before You.

33 ✓
My God,
how could I be disappointed while You are my hope,
or how could I be betrayed while my trust is in You?

34
My God,
how can I deem myself exalted
while You have planted me in lowliness,
or why should I *not* deem myself exalted,
for You have related me to Yourself?
Why should I not be in need of You,
for You have set me up in poverty,
or why should I be needy,
for You have enriched me with Your goodness?
Apart from You there is no God.
You have made Yourself known to everything
so nothing is ignorant of You.
And it is You who have made Yourself known to me in
everything;
thus, I have seen You manifest *in* everything,
and You are the Manifest *to* everything.
O He who betakes Himself to His throne
with His All-Mercifulness,
so that the throne is hidden in His All-Mercifulness,

just as the Universe is hidden in His throne,
You have annihilated created things with created things,
and obliterated alterities with the all-encompassing spheres of
light![164]
O He who, in His pavilions of glory,
is veiled from the reach of sight,
O He who illumines with the perfection of His Beauty
and whose Infinity is realized by the gnostics' innermost
being—
how can You be hidden, for You are the Exterior?[165]
Or how can You be absent,
for You are the Ever-Present Watcher?

God is the Granter of Success—and in Him I take refuge!

Notes

1. One should be detached toward one's actions, not attached to their positive or negative fruits. We must rely on the Divinity, not on our own actions or deeds. According to one of the commentators, the person who relies on God suffers no diminution of hope when he falls into disobedience nor does his hope increase when he performs a virtuous deed.

2. The word for "isolation" in Arabic is *tajrid*, which carries with it the implication of withdrawing from society for contemplative aims, the one doing so being called a *mutajarrid*, whereas the one who carries on his contemplative life within society is the *mutasabbib*, that is to say, he is concerned also with his livelihood *(sabab)* in the world.

3. It is not a matter of choice, it is a question of vocation, predetermined by the general tendencies of the individual. One might add that the spiritual master *(Shaykh)* of a Sufi order likewise controls the eventual orientation of the *faqir*.

4. Whatever might be one's prior intentions or aspirations *(himam,* plural of *himmah)*, they cannot set aside what Destiny has decreed must take place. The anteriority in time of the intention is likened to an arrow, as it were, that cannot pierce the walls of Destiny, which represent the fixity of predestined Decrees. Nevertheless, the gnostic's intention or aspiration can be so strong for a given thing that it coincides with the divine Will, which actualizes it immediately, according to Ibn 'Ajibah, one of the commentators.

5. Self-direction *(tadbir)* implies egocentric concern for one's direction in life, and more particularly in one's daily existence, to the point where it blots out the obligations due to God. In that case, the *tadbir* is negative and should be eliminated. But if the planning or direction is in conjunction with the directives of God, then it is positive and not an obstacle in the Path, in which case it is not self-direction, or an egocentric manifestation, but Self-direction, which is not in the least individualistic. It is not so much that all future planning should be set to one side as it is that one should repose in the knowledge that one's future has been taken care of by providential arrangements: One has but to flow into the divine mould that has already been prepared.

6. This is similar to what Hikmah no. 4 points to, but it carries things a step further. The seeker's livelihood in this world is already guaranteed to him by Providence: One should flow along with it without undue strain. If such strain is present and forces the seeker to be remiss in his

obligations, such as the daily rituals, his discernment is eventually curtailed.

7. The "Gift" is the celestial response to the *faqir*, the "sign" that he is making headway.

8. Both no. 6 and no. 7 treat of the same thing: one must not give way to despair or doubt if things do not go according to one's own choice, for this can cloud the inner eye of the heart.

9. There is no common measure between the insignificant deeds of the traveler in the Path and the immense results obtained at its end. God may suddenly intervene with intrusions of Self-revelation that seem disproportionately great in relation to the deeds of the individual.

10. Inspiration (*warid*) affects the spiritual state (*hal*) of the soul in terms of expansion, contraction, intimacy with God, and the like; but these are all interior states of being that nevertheless manifest themselves in exterior actions. These actions are the expressions, necessarily varied, of the different interior states.

11. Actions untouched by sincerity, in the spiritual sense of that term, are dead forms; but let sincerity penetrate them and it is as if the Spirit had brought life into them.

12. The "earth of obscurity" here is self-effacement, the opposite of all individualism that bloats the ego.

13. Meditation *(fikrah)* is a kind of flow of thoughts on the attributes of the Absolute that introduces a state of concentration in the mind, thus purifying it and allowing its deeper layers of luminosity to rise to the surface.

14. The "heart" is not only the luminous center where the ray of the Spirit meets the plane of the soul, but also, in fallen man, it is the seat of passions, sentiments, and ignorance. The combat that takes place in the contemplative life is between the transcendent Spirit and the egocentric soul, to determine which shall govern the heart. To the extent that the Spirit prevails, the heart is illumined. The polishing of the mirror of the heart, a favorite expression in Sufism, involves cleansing it of all that is other-than-God. Man's fallen nature covers or veils the eye of the heart, which is the Spirit, with multiplicity, or "the forms of creatures," preventing its inherent luminosity from radiating throughout the soul. This entire Hikmah points out the contradictions in those who would unite with God while still subject to the effects of the Fall (*al-hubut*).

15. The darkness of the Cosmos symbolizes its nonexistence, its nothingness. Whatever exists, therefore, derives its being from God, the origin of all things. Not to see this unique divine Source behind the multiplicity of things implies the "veiling" of one's intelligence: So long as this

veiling persists, the eye of the heart (*'ayn al-qalb*) cannot function normally and the solar nature of gnosis (*ma'rifah*) cannot shine forth from one's inner being. Note the equation of darkness with nothingness, light with existence or being.

16. The Omnipotence of the Divinity is Its creative art that has the power to bring the entire universe into being while at the same time effecting an apparent separation between the Creator and the Creation, a separation that is only illusory in the sense that it is not absolutely so. Without the divine Omnipotence, the world could not have come into being; without the separative tendency, the Real (*al-Haqq*) and the Creation (*al-Khalq*) would not be distinct; but this distinction is only relatively true, for they are essentially identical. That being so, the idea that the Creation—as a cosmos or universe—has a separate reality alongside that of the Real is an illusion, a "veiling," a failure to perceive things with the eye of the heart, for there cannot be two ultimate Realities, which would be contrary to the basic Islamic thesis of *tawhid*, the affirmation of the Oneness of the Absolute, *Allah*. To affirm that there is something that has coexistence with God in an absolute manner is to fall into *shirk*, or "associationism," which is to assert that *Allah*, who is One, has associates or partners or peers. Still, the power of the world to veil the individual from God derives from the divine Omnipotence itself, which could not but bring into existence a world that is other-than-God, which has "no existence alongside of Him."

17. This Hikmah proceeds to smash the illusion mentioned in no. 15, except that the origin of the veiling there is in God's Omnipotence, whereas here the origin is in the individual as such, who does not see that nothing whatsoever can veil the One. One of the ninety-nine Names of the Divinity in Islam is *az-Zahir* ("the Exterior," "the Manifest"), which is the opposite of another Name, *al-Batin* ("the Interior," "the Unmanifest"). This Hikmah takes the entire world as proceeding from the reality of the Name *az-Zahir*. Nothing could be more manifest than the Manifest, who is God.

18. If there were something alongside of Him, He would not be the One, for there would then be two realities, or three, or four, and so forth. Not to see the One in all things, in all multiplicity, is spiritual *shirk* and therefore the opposite of *tawhid*. Let us recall that *shirk* is the cardinal sin in Islam, although it is true that, on the exoteric plane of the Law, it is not defined in the esoteric Sufi sense, which has in view its contemplative and spiritual and even metaphysical ramifications and consequences, whereas in ordinary Islam *shirk* has to do with polytheism in the paganistic sense, *tawhid* being the affirmation of *Allah* as the One and the rejection of idols. One can see that in exoteric Islam a mild or even serious form of spiritual *shirk* can exist alongside the official *tawhid*; and it is no doubt for this reason that Sufism, making no concessions to hypocritical tendencies, insists on

total *tawhid*, with no residues of *shirk* lurking in the human psyche to act as blocks to the contemplative life. Sufi esoterism is the sacred science of total *tawhid*, whereas Islamic exoterism is but fragmentary *tawhid*: This is the difference between the Path (*tariqah*) and the Law (*shari'ah*) as generally understood by the Sufis, who nevertheless recognize that both emanate from the same Reality (*Haqiqah*). Sufism pictures the *Haqiqah* as the central point in a circle; the radius connecting the point to the circle is the *tariqah*; the circle itself is the *shari'ah*. One cannot tread the Path without the Law, the latter providing an initial and provisional version of *tawhid* which the Path (i.e., Sufism) will deepen until the contemplative sees "the One alongside of whom there is nothing," as our Hikmah puts it.

19. The Qur'an affirms that God is nearer to man than his jugular vein, and in this Hikmah that imagery is assumed. One of the Names of the Divinity in Islam is "the Near" (*al-Qarib*); such being the case, there can be nothing that is "nearer" than He is.

20. This Hikmah draws attention to the mysterious interconnections between God and the world—the Absolute and the relative, Being and nonbeing, and so forth; but note that, for the author, the mystery is not in God so much as it is in the world, that derives whatever being it has from the pure Being of *Allah*, who alone is Real, everything else being illusory. The author is marveling at the illusory nature of the world, which "is" and "is not," depending on how one looks at it. This ambiguity of the world derives from its nature as other-than-God.

21. To oppose Destiny or Fate is to oppose the divine Will, which is ignorance, whereas, according to the commentators, whatever happens in oneself or in the world around one is what God wills. It is a question here of what the Sufis call "the instant" (*al-waqt*), as the commentator Ahmad Zarruq points out: Whoever submits to His decision at that moment is saved; whoever opposes it by abandoning contentment and satisfaction with the divine Will at that instant suffers a fall or a relapse, so that, from an intellectual point of view, he manifests his ignorance also by desiring that a "fact" that has occurred be reversed, which is the same as desiring the impossible! Obviously, the author is saying, whatever appears in a given moment or instant is a fact that has to be accepted in the knowledge that it proceeds from the divine Will operating in every instant. The Sufi, by the way, is "the son of the instant," or *Ibn al-Waqt*, which means that he lives in the "present," not in the past or in the future; he lives in the here and now.

22. In view of what was said in Hikmah no. 17 about the moment and what no. 209 says about the irreplaceable past and the priceless present, this particular Hikmah alludes to the illusory nature of all procrastination, for, as Ibn 'Ajibah points out, death may supervene!

23. One must accept whatever state God puts one in, more or less in

the spirit of no. 17, as Ibn 'Abbad says; but he adds that this does not include the transgression of commands on the part of an individual, since this is a different question altogether.

24. Qur'an 2:102, for this last citation; the other one in the text is of the author's own composition. In other words, the early fruits of the Path do not constitute the end; there is still more to come. The exterior beauties, or charms, of things are only indicative of their interior realities, that are much more "real." One must push on further and further in the process of interiorization and not stop at external forms.

25. This does not mean that the servant ('abd) should not petition God for this or that; rather, he should not do so while thinking that he has been neglected, for he is constantly under surveillance. Nor should one betake oneself to creatures with the idea of seeking their aid, as if somehow this aid were apart from God's help, or as if this seeking could be accomplished with flattery and hypocrisy. On the contrary, His intervention operates in all domains; hence, one must be aware of this at all moments, and being aware of this, one must maintain a correct attitude toward God and toward one's fellowman.

26. This by way of instilling the notion that all depends on the divine Will, including such apparently insignificant things as the breaths of man, which are limited in number, as Ibn 'Ajibah says, so that when one's alloted number of breaths comes to an end, there ends one's life as one moves on to the Hereafter. If the breaths are counted, he asks, then what about one's steps, one's thoughts, and everything else?

27. The word "alterities" (al-aghyar) is a technical Sufi expression implying multiplicity and as such is characteristic of other-than-God, that is to say, it is the world insofar as it preoccupies the heart and prevents it from being exclusively attentive to the divine Presence. The world being multiple by its very nature, there is no point in looking forward to being free of its attractive pull; rather, one should be vigilantly attentive now to the Presence in the heart, for that is what really counts.

28. This Hikmah is related to no. 23, for it spells out the nature of the world, which is not God. Not being, on its own plane, the Divinity, it is necessarily compounded of joys and sorrows; God alone is pure bliss. Useless is it, then, to lament its nature, which is imperfection, the imperfection of the other-than-God. To want it to be perfect with the perfection of God is to seek for two absolute perfections; but this is shirk.

29. Ibn 'Abbad says that every seeker has a beginning and an end. The beginning has to do with his voyaging, which implies turning to God; the end has to do with his arriving, which implies his union with God. If he is illumined to turn to God in the beginning, he will be illumined in his union with God at the end; if he does not turn to God in the beginning and

relies instead on other-than-He, he will not be illumined.

30. The external forms mirror the internal essences; what a person has in his heart is manifested outwardly in his face and body, according to Ibn 'Abbad. It is not simply a question of his positive qualities, as Ibn 'Ajibah would put it, but also of his negative traits, his vices, which show themselves with the same clarity and can be "read" by the person who has the discernment of forms.

31. Gnosis takes its point of departure with the Real (*al-Haqq*, which also means "the Truth" and "God" and is one of the ninety-nine Names of *Allah*), not with the Creation (*al-Khalq*), which is, from the usual point of view, other-than-God; it thus works downward to the world from God, not upward from the world to God. It is theologians, philosophers, and others who argue syllogistically from the imperfection of things to the Perfection of God, from multiplicity (*al-athar*) to the divine Unity, and from the relativity of everything to the Absolute. But their argumentation is defective, for God is not "absent" at any given moment that one has to "prove" Him inferentially, nor is He so distant that it is via created things or multiplicity that one must "reach" Him. On the contrary, He is present and near—He is "here" and "now." We should start with Him, not with the world. Ibn 'Ajibah, in commenting on this Hikmah, mentions the two groups as being, on the one hand, the people of love, who have gnosis, sanctity, and direct vision, and, on the other hand, the people of service, who stop at the external shells and have no light of knowledge or understanding.

32. Qur'an 65:7.

33. Ibid. Those who have reached the end of the Path are blessed with graces and knowledge that they diffuse among others spontaneously; those who are voyaging do not have this superabundance of spiritual wealth. Ahmad Zarruq equates the two groups with the two mentioned in Hikmah no. 29: The sage who is united with God proceeds from Him; the initiate still voyaging toward God proceeds inferentially to Him.

34. Qur'an 6:92. This Hikmah really continues the previous themes—those who have the lights of confrontation being those who are united with God; those who have the lights of orientation being those voyaging toward Him. Ibn 'Ajibah takes the three stations of Islam, namely, *islam* ("submission"), *iman* ("faith"), and *ihsan* ("spiritual virtue"), as found in the famous *hadith* of the Prophet, and divides them up between the two groups. The lights of orientation, accordingly, are the lights associated with the stations of *islam* and *iman*, whereas the lights of confrontation are those associated with the station of *ihsan*. He does much the same thing for other well-known Sufi ternaries, such as "the Law, the Path, the Reality" (*ash-shari'ah, at-tariqah, al-Haqiqah*), where the first two belong to the lights

of orientation, the last one to the lights of confrontation.

35. Ahmad Zarruq says that it is in the nature of the ego to ignore vices and to seek hidden things, whereas it is the opposite that should be done.

36. Qur'an 6:18. God being Infinite, nothing can limit him, for there are not two Infinites. The Real cannot therefore be veiled by anything whatsoever; it is the individual who is veiled; his fallen nature has led him to believe that "something" can veil the Real, but this is an illusion. One should read this Hikmah while keeping in mind the words of Hikmah nos. 15 and 16. Shaykh Ibn 'Ajibah cites the words of his own master in explanation of this Hikmah: "Nothing but illusion (al-wahm) veils mankind from God, but illusion is an inexistent matter—it has no reality."

37. A triad of technical terminology is found here: shu'a' al-basirah ("the ray of light of the intellect"), 'ayn al-basirah ("the eye of the intellect"), and Haqq al-basirah ("the Truth of the intellect"). These three correspond to another ternary, as pointed out by Ibn 'Ajibah in his commentary: 'ilm al-yaqin ("the knowledge of certitude"), which is really theoretical doctrine; 'ayn al-yaqin ("the eye of certitude"), which has to do with those progressing in the Path and who have more than just theoretical insight; and Haqq al-yaqin ("the Truth of certitude"), which has to do with those who have reached the end of the Path and possess the Truth through contemplation and direct vision. Ibn 'Ajibah also points to a hierarchic correspondence between the ternary mentioned in the Hikmah and another well-known ternary: the 'Alam al-Mulk ("the World of the Kingdom"), which is the physical world of existence and corresponds to the eye of the intellect; the 'Alam al-Malakut ("the World of the Realm"), the world of immaterial, pyschic realities, of the world soul, which corresponds to the eye of the intellect; and the 'Alam al-Jabarut ("the World of absolute Sovereignty"), which is the highest of the three worlds and corresponds to the domain of spiritual realities, where the Spirit is to be found, beyond the soul. There is, accordingly, a relationship, easily perceived, between these ternaries and the one mentioned in the footnote to Hikmah no. 31, namely, the Law, the Path, and the divine Reality (shari'ah, tariqah, Haqiqah). In all of these a hierarchic progression can be seen; in this particular Hikmah, the beginning, middle, and end of the contemplative path are traced out. Let us recall that the Truth in such phrases as "the Truth of the intellect" does not refer merely to a mental or conceptual image but rather to God as the ultimate Real independent of man and his thinking—the Real (al-Haqq) in Itself.

38. Sometimes this Hikmah is united with the previous one by way of describing the Truth of the intellect, the last stage of the Path, which implies the realization that there is nothing outside the Real. The Hikmah is really a hadith except that the phrase "and He is now as He was" is consi-

dered to be an addition. The *hadith* posits the absoluteness of the Real in Itself, without associates; and it implies the nothingness of other-than-God, a nothingness that is not merely a figure of speech, as one might be tempted to think.

39. Qur'an 22:46. By the "heart" is meant the clouded intelligence that does not discern the relativity of the world and its impermanence and that the Decrees of Destiny cannot be eluded: There is blindness in such a heart.

40. Qur'an 53:42. The person occupied with creatures and not with the Creator is trapped in multiplicity, and round and round he goes, without exit. The *hadith* of the Prophet that is cited in the text points out the importance of intention (*niyyah*): One must deepen it, with God in view.

41. Qur'an 14:20. The Invocation (*dhikr*) in question is the primary spiritual means of realization in Sufism, the basic technique of concentration. It is the Invocation, inwardly or outwardly, of a Name of the Divinity in Islam, and especially of the supreme Name, *Allah;* under the guidance of a teacher, the Invocation becomes a permanent "prayer of the heart." The author describes herein, somewhat succinctly, different initiatic stages of the Invocation. Called the *dhikru 'llah* ("the Invocation of *Allah*"), this Sufi method of concentration brings to mind the *Japa-yoga* of Hinduism, the Jesus Prayer of the Hesychastic tradition of the Eastern Church, and the *Nembutsu* of Japan, all of which use a divine Name that is to be invoked, the goal being to concentrate on it permanently.

42. Inspiration is called *warid* (plural is *waridat*), and is defined by Shaykh Ibn 'Ajibah in his commentary on this Hikmah as "a divine light that God casts in the heart of the one He loves among His servants." Inspirations, for Ibn 'Ajibah, are of three types: inspirations that occur at the beginning of the Path, those that occur in the middle, and those that occur at the end, when union has taken place.

43. The lights mentioned here are spiritual in nature and coincide with the "inspirations" (*al-waridat*), and must not be confused with psychic lights in the soul nor even less with physical lights. The term *sirr* (plural is *asrar*) means the innermost center or being of an individual, much more subtle, says Ibn 'Ajibah, than "heart" (*qalb*), but both refer to one and the same thing, namely, the Spirit (*ar-Ruh*); and he goes on to say that when the Spirit is purified completely and turns back to its origin in God it is called "mystery" (*sirr*).

44. The word *qalb* means "heart" and also, as a verbal noun, inverting or reversing, a turning inside out or outside in; thus, the heart can both progress in the Path and retrogress, depending on case.

45. Qur'an 10:58. We can do nothing without the grace of God.

46. The term *al-wahm* is polyvalent in signification and can mean

"illusion," "suspicion," "self-deception," and the like. Here it is the delusion that mankind has the power to harm or benefit and must be treated with flattery or other attitudes that lead to covetousness. Shaykh Ahmad Zarruq interprets *al-wahm* in the sense of imagination that causes an individual to fall into coveting. The following Hikmah speaks of the enslavement brought on by covetousness.

47. Qur'an 7:182. This is more fully explained in the next Hikmah (no. 66).

48. Qur'an 17:20. Nos. 67 and 68 deal with the universality of God's providential care for His servants.

49. Ibn 'Abbad says that the pleasure and felicity encountered in performing good deeds are their immediate fruits and are the signs of God's accepting such deeds.

50. Shaykh Ahmad Zarruq says that what God seeks from man is three things: emptying oneself of everything except Him; adorning oneself with what pleases Him; perserverance in both without letup or shortcoming till "you meet Him."

51. Ibn 'Abbad explains that the real gnostic would not be concerned with his symbolic allusion to begin with, since that would be involvement with what is other-than-God; and he has no symbolic allusion because of his extinction in God.

52. Contraction and expansion (*qabd* and *bast*) are purely spiritual states of being that befall the heart (*al-qalb*), according to Ahmad Zarruq, so that at times it is contracted, at times expanded, at times it is equilibrated. These states are in themselves spiritual but do have psychological repercussions in the soul, such as sadness and joy. They are alternating states along the Path, similar in their succession to the cycles of days and nights. Contraction is related to the fear of God, expansion to hope in God; but there are states beyond these.

53. Once again, as in no. 20, he draws attention to the exterior and interior aspect of things, the soul or the ego attaching itself to the exterior forms, the heart or the intelligence going straight to their interior essences.

54. Ibn 'Abbad says that when the light of certitude shines in the heart of a servant, the world is extinguished in his sight and is folded up in his thinking, and he sees the Hereafter present before him. Compare this Hikmah with no. 13, which develops another aspect of the same theme.

55. God's recompense, as Shaykh Ibn 'Abbad puts it, is not only in the Hereafter but also in this world—and now—for those servants whom He wishes to encourage in their efforts.

56. Ibn 'Ajibah comments that the seeker may flag during his voyage to the Divinity and become tired out in his striving; his ego overcomes him, as a result, and he commits a sin, which results in his downfall; but when he

rises from this fall, he could have such renewed dedication that it would take him all the way to the divine Presence. He cites the *hadith*: "Many a sin has caused its perpetrator to enter Paradise!" When asked to explain how this could be, the Prophet, in speaking of the sinner and his sin, answered: "He never ceases being repentant over it, fleeing from it, and fearing his Lord, till he dies—and it causes him to enter Paradise!"

57. Man is totally dependent for his continued existence on God in an essential manner, as was pointed out in nos. 97 and 98. The two graces of "existence" and "sustenance" are absolutely necessary; if they were withdrawn, we would be reduced to nothingness; hence our indigence is total. The "accidents" referred to are such things as well-being, health, or the trials that come over us, such as illness and suffering, which are but reminders of the essential indigence that we tend to ignore.

58. It never vanishes because he knows that he is nothing by virtue of his gnosis that reveals to him the absoluteness of God; nor can he repose in anyone or anything but God for there is nothing "outside" of God.

59. The "lights of His created things" are the sun and the moon; the "uncreated lights of His attributes" are the divine qualities, such as Majesty, Beauty, Sublimity, and the like, according to Ibn 'Ajibah. The Sun of hearts is the immanent Spirit that gnosis unveils.

60. As the commentators say, the ways leading to God have been very clearly expounded; however, passion can overcome the mind, leading to blindness that impedes progress in the Path; and that is what is feared.

61. The "inner reality of holiness" (*sirr al-khususiyyah*), as explained by Ibn 'Ajibah, is the Light of the Truth in the hearts of those saintly servants of God who have been purified of all stain. Perfected human nature is like a sanctuary or a temple enveloping that interior holiness. "Lordship" (*rububiyyah*) has to do with the quality of God as Lord of the Creation, with all that this implies in the way of attributes; "servanthood" (*'ubudiyyah*) is its complementary term, and refers to man's attitudes as the creature or servant of God, the gnostic being the perfect "servant."

62. As Ibn 'Ajibah puts it, not everyone who manifests miracles or charismatic signs (which would be, by the way, indications of his being among the chosen) has already achieved liberation from his imperfections and faults. These charismatic signs might come over him, according to Ibn 'Ajibah, for three reasons: to encourage him after a period of lassitude; to test him to see whether he will stand still or go further; to increase his certitude or the certitude of someone else in him.

63. There is a play on words here, litany being *wird* and inspiration *warid*, both coming from the same consonantal roots.

64. Ibn 'Ajibah explains that "sustenance" here means the lights of orientation for the voyagers and the lights of confrontation for those who

are united with God (see Hikmah no. 31), the sustenance being for the sake of the purification of the heart.

65. Devotees (*'ubbad*) and ascetics (*zuhhad*) are distinguished in this Hikmah from the gnostics (*'arifun*). As Ibn 'Ajibah explains, the devotees are distracted from God by the sweetness of their devotions; the ascetics are distracted from God by their acts of asceticism; the gnostics see the Real in all things and hence are never absent from God.

66. Ibn 'Abbad points out that the acquisition of gnosis leads to permanent company with God, which in turn requires permanent contemplation; knowing that His servant has that contemplative state, God reveals to him His creatures and created things that issue from Him, as forms to be contemplated, and all this as a "relaxation" to His servant

67. "Ritual prayer" must be distinguished from the Invocation (*dhikr*); the Qur'an states that the Invocation of *Allah* is greater than ritual prayer. Ritual prayer refers to the five daily prayers binding on all Muslims by the Law of Islam, and as such it is one of the Pillars of the religion, the others being the Testimony of Faith (*shahadah*), the Pilgrimage (*hajj*), fasting during the month of Ramadan (*siyam Ramadan*), and the legal alms (*zakat*); occasionally, a sixth Pillar, Holy War (*jihad*), is added. Ritual prayer (*salat*) occurs at specific moments during the course of the day (see Hikmah no. 194 on this matter) and is accordingly in stark contrast with the uninterrupted nature of the *dhikr*.

68. As Shaykh Ahmad Zarruq points out, the doer of one's acts is God, the unique Agent; to seek recompense for a deed performed by Him is bad manners. See Hikmah no. 72 for the question of God's "acceptance" of deeds.

69. God's grace is supreme, says Ibn 'Abbad, so when He wants to manifest it to a servant He creates obedience within him and makes it sweet to him; then He attributes that obedience to the servant.

70. There is a play here on the word "habits" (*'awa'id*) and "laws of nature" (*'awa'id*): Islam considers miracles as ruptures of the laws of nature or of the "habits" of nature. So long as one's own bad habits have not been eliminated, it is useless to aspire to perform miracles.

71. An important Hikmah, it announces the incommensurable nature of spiritual realization: There can be no common measure between the individual's efforts to unite with the Absolute and the eventual results. It is the Infinite itself that intervenes within the finite to effect the union.

72. It is rare, says Ibn 'Ajibah, that the deeds of man be impregnated with sincerity; thus, God veils our imperfections in deeds through His kindly veiling and accepts them, however tarnished they might be.

73. Because, as Ahmad Zarruq explains, obedience can lead to self-

satisfaction, whereas disobedience leads to self-negation and the awareness that one is in need of God.

74. The beauty of God's veiling, according to Ibn 'Ajibah, is that he providentially covers His servant's imperfections with His qualities; consequently, whatever good qualities are in him do not belong to him.

75. Here the doctrine of illusion is presented to account for the veiling often mentioned in the book and in other Sufi works. See Hikmah no. 33 for a similar statement.

76. Without His bringing beings and things into existence, there would have been no Creation whatsoever (no macrocosm), and thus there would have been no perception of things by an individual (no microcosm). Had His Qualities been manifested in a pure state, instead of being progressively veiled by the degrees of reality as they descended down into our world, the Creation would have been annihilated.

77. As stated previously, the words "the Interior" (al-Batin) and "the Exterior" (az-Zahir) are two of the ninety-nine Names of Allah and are drawn from the Qur'an: "He is the First and the Last and the Exterior and the Interior" (57:3). This is one of the richest verses of the Qur'an and has often been used by the Sufis. God is the First "before" the Creation, just as He will be the Last after the Creation has been reabsorbed, or "after" the Creation. A spatial symbolism and a temporal symbolism are implied in the verse: The First and the Last suggest a circle closing in on its initial point of origin; the Interior and the Exterior suggest a central point and an outer circle or sphere. The Creation is manifested because He is the Interior, the hidden Source from which all manifestation proceeds. On the other hand, the Creation is hidden because He is the Exterior, or the Manifest, more manifest or more real than the symbolic nature of the world that points to Him. The exterior world, it should not be forgotten, is not the Exterior in Itself, but only a symbol of it on a different plane, otherwise it would be the same thing, which would be equivalent to abolishing the degrees of reality or of reducing everything created to its Principle. In the latter case, there would be no exterior world at all, but only "the Exterior" or "the Manifest," that is ontologically prior to the Creation. As Hikmah no. 16 says, in one of its many questions: "How can it be conceived that something veils Him, since He was the Manifest *before* the existence of anything?"

78. Qur'an 10:101. We meet again the distinction between the interior and exterior aspects of things, as we see in nos. 20 and 85. We must not stop at the forms of things, for they will imprison us if we do, and instead we must go straight to their essences, since these alone liberate our minds.

79. There are two perspectives here, depending on the point of departure. There is, first of all, the perspective of existence as such: The world

exists because it derives its reality from God, its Existentiator, its ontological Principle, without which it could not exist at all. Then there is, secondly, the perspective of the Principle as such: The world "is not" in any way whatsoever because there is nothing "outside" or "alongside" the divine Unity. On the one hand, the world is relatively real; on the other hand, it is unreal, or even nothing at all, for only the divine Unity is the Real (al-Haqq). One should not forget these two positions in trying to grasp our author's ideas; at times, he situates himself in one viewpoint, at times in another.

80. Qur'an 4:11. Compare this aphorism with no. 81. Note the equation of night with contraction and day with expansion.

81. The "lights" in question, says Ibn 'Ajibah, are the "inspirations" (al-waridat) and "revelations" (al-kushufat) that remove all veils. The distinction made in the Hikmah between "hearts" (al-qulub) and "innermost centers of being" (al-asrar) is one of degree; but ultimately, according to Shaykh Ibn 'Ajibah, terms such as "heart" (qalb), intelligence ('aql), Spirit (Ruh), and Mystery or Secret (Sirr)—the last-named being the innermost center of being—are one and the same thing. The "lights" mentioned in this Hikmah and in nos. 152–155 are of course spiritual lights, not psychic or physical lights; the last-named are the ones that unveil the sensorial world around us. Ibn 'Ajibah, in speaking of the spiritual lights, classifies them according to a threefold division: First comes the weakest light, which is the light of the station of "submission" (islam), and resembles the faint light of the stars; then comes the stronger light, which is the light of the station of "faith" (iman), like the light of the moon; and finally comes the strongest light of all, which is the light of the station of "spiritual virtue" (ihsan), like the light of the sun. One might point out in passing, as did Ibn 'Ajibah in his commentary, that the ternary islam-iman-ihsan, in that order, is common to Sufism, whereas in exoteric Islam the progression is given as iman-islam-ihsan due to the dictum of the doctors of the Law that nothing is valid without "faith" preceding it.

82. The distinction is between sensorial light and intelligible light. The latter light is divisible into the three types mentioned in note 81.

83. See Hikmah no. 108 for another version of the same truth.

84. The "saints" mentioned here are the Shaykhs of the Path. Providence guides the seeker to the Shaykh so that ultimately he be united with God. The sign leading to the sage is the sign leading to God.

85. The particular distinction (khususiyyah), says Ibn 'Ajibah, might be asceticism, piety, a miracle, a gnostic intuition, and the like; but if, after receiving it, you should want others to know of it, then this is proof of a secret hypocrisy and of insincerity toward God.

86. The "nearness" mentioned has nothing to do with spatial distance,

as Ibn 'Abbad points out, but rather has to do with the encompassing nature of His Knowledge, Power, and Will.

87. The prior giving, as interpreted by Ibn 'Ajibah, is related to His eternal Knowledge before creatures were brought into being; and because all of the "giving" and the "depriving" has been settled from all Eternity, one's subsequent asking cannot be the cause of God's giving.

88. Ahmad Zarruq gives the reason for this by saying that secondary or contingent causes are created and posterior, while the nature of Eternity is that it is anterior, with nothing preceding it.

89. In Eternity, there is no "you," as Ibn 'Abbad puts it; thus, His providential care of the individual could not be caused by anything coming from him; he had not yet been created and was a pure nothingness.

90. Qur'an 2:105.

91. Qur'an 7:56. Since the care of Providence over its creatures is "already" settled, each one naturally sits back awaiting its emergence in himself; but the Qur'anic phrase clearly indicates that God chooses this or that person for His Mercy, thus excluding some from His providential care. Lest that provoke a general indifference and abandonment of effort, the Qur'an pinpoints those who fall under the care of Providence (or Mercy, which amounts to the same thing), namely, "the doers of good."

92. Creatures are subject to the Will of God, but His Will is not subject to anything in the Creation. A clarification having to do with asking, however, is in order at this point. One's asking takes place in the temporal world, but the giving has been fixed from all Eternity, "before" one asked. Thus, as he says in no. 168, a contingent thing such as asking cannot be the cause of His giving, for in Eternity, which has nothing to do with time, past or future, there is only "pure bestowing" and "sublime giving" (no. 169). This cannot be construed as a rejection on his part of asking, for he has said in no. 166 that one should ask for the sake of showing one's servanthood and fulfilling the rights due to God as Lord, or as possessor of Lordship. Moreover, by way of completing the picture, one's asking is itself subject to the divine Will, as he points out in this Hikmah, when he says that everything depends on the divine Will, which of course would include one's asking.

93. According to a *hadith* cited by the commentators, the Divinity is pictured as saying through the mouth of the Prophet these words: "He whose invocation of Me distracts him from asking Me—to him will I give the best of what is given to the askers."

94. Nos. 174–178 all deal with the question of spiritual poverty. The "need" or "indigence" of the novice is essential (no. 99); the need is a matter of self-effacement before God.

95. Qur'an 9:60. The "feast-days" and "gifts" mentioned in nos. 174

and 177 are all the fruits of the Path, such as intuitions, blessings, virtues, and wisdom. These come to the degree that the ego is extinguished by poverty of the Spirit.

96. Ibn 'Ajibah points out that the attributes of "servanthood" (*ubudiyyah*) are four, to which correspond four attributes of "Lordship" (*rububiyyah*) in God. The four in the servant are poverty of Spirit, lowliness, impotence, and weakness; the four in God are Wealth, Sublimity, Power, and Strength.

97. Miracles can occur at the hands of someone who has yet to perfect himself spiritually, remarks Ibn 'Abbad, but the true miracle is the transformation of one's nature and the extinction of the ego.

98. The "fruits," according to Ibn 'Ajibah, are the virtues, the fulfilling of the rights due to God, and the like.

99. There are two groups, explains Ibn 'Ajibah—those who are veiled, and those who are unveiled. The first are the doctors of the Law, the second are the gnostics. When someone from the first group makes a mistake, he is silenced out of shame before God or fear of Him; when someone in the second group makes a mistake, he is not silenced because the misbehavior comes from himself whereas his expression comes from God; and indeed, this is only a way of speaking about the second group, for they witness only the behavior of God in themselves and hence their misbehavior could not silence them, for they are drowned in an ocean of graces and see nothing but Him in the world.

100. From Hikmah 183 to 188, the discussion revolves around the permission (*idhn*) that the Sufi sages receive to teach the Path to disciples. This particular Hikmah establishes the general rule that a person's speech betrays what he has in his heart and that it will affect others accordingly.

101. The latter case is that of the Shaykhs of the Path.

102. The "insight" here belongs to the person who has realization.

103. Ibn 'Abbad explains that he should not express them to anyone except his Shaykh. To express them is to give vent to his egocentric tendencies.

104. Ibn 'Abbad says that people are divided into two camps, as far as their daily nourishment is concerned: those who work for their nourishment and those who do not work for it but receive it instead at the hands of creatures. In this Hikmah, only the second group is mentioned and two conditions are imposed for taking things from others: that God be seen as the true Giver, and that the taking be done under the control of knowledge. In general, the commentators see in this Hikmah a reference to those who are subject to a life of mendicancy, those who live in "isolation" (*tajrid*), not to those who live in the world, working with their own hands to make a living.

NOTES

105. As Ibn 'Ajibah puts it, the gnostic sees only the Real and is in any case so near his Lord that he is ashamed to ask Him for something other-than-He. All the more would his shame be if he were to address himself to another creature of His!

106. This Hikmah is explained by no. 192, since obligatory deeds are those that weigh on the ego.

107. The five daily ritual prayers fall within specific times, as was said previously, but each prayer has a time span that permits the pious to choose within it their own moment of performing the prayer.

108. This is a *hadith* of the Prophet.

109. Qur'an 18:45.

110. The graces that come upon the seeker, from the grace of faith to the grace of guidance in the Path, should not go unrecognized, states Ibn 'Ajibah, even if that recognition be in the form of a simple expression praising God.

111. The "unsettling fear" has to do with the divine Majesty, which forces the novice to abandon his particular passion; the "restless desire" has to do with the divine Beauty, which creates an attractive force that pulls him out of his earthbound passion and directs him upward.

112. The affirmation of the Oneness of God (*tawhid*) demands increasing sincerity in the *faqir*: The false gods in him must go. The deed that is associationist is the one performed without God in view; the heart that is associationist is the one that loves other-than-God.

113. Ibn 'Ajibah, in explaining this Hikmah, says that the lights allowed to arrive are the lights of "faith" (*iman*); the lights that enter are the lights of "spiritual virtue" (*ihsan*). The person who has the former lights is not altogether devoid of worldly tendencies; the person who has the latter lights is devoid of all alterities. One will note that the author does not speak here of any lights belonging to the people of "submission" (*islam*), perhaps because it is only at the degree of faith (*iman*) that one can start speaking of "lights" properly so-called, or of real lights in a lofty sense.

114. See Hikmah no. 13, which asks: "How can the heart be illumined while the forms of creatures are reflected in its mirror?"

115. Ibn 'Ajibah says that union with God is through the actualization of knowledge of His Being by absence from one's self and from all that which is other-than-God. It is therefore not a question of material or sensorial union with God in a pantheistic sense.

116. Qur'an 75:18–19. Inspirations arrive synthetically. It is only after retention or assimilation that their explanation can be detailed. The Qur'anic verse cited is addressed to the Prophet and refers to the revelation of the Qur'an.

117. Qur'an 27:34.

118. Qur'an 21:18. Divine inspirations have a purifying effect on the soul; they are also illuminative, since they destroy illusions and falsehood.

119. Still another repetition of a theme that runs throughout the book, namely, that nothing veils God, as we find, for example, in Hikmah no. 16.

120. See nos. 52–54 for other developments of this Hikmah on inspirations and their purposes.

121. Because if one had found Him, as Shaykh Ahmad Zarruq says, then all that is other-than-He would be of no moment, and if one were united to Him, then the intimacy that results would suffice against the feeling of estrangement at other-than-He.

122. According to Ibn 'Ajibah, this Hikmah has to do with the post-humous states, the felicity being the contemplation of the Lord, and the suffering being the veiling that impedes that contemplation.

123. Worries and sadnesses, in the opinion of Ibn 'Abbad, come from self-consciousness; once this goes, inner vision is possible.

124. The term "post" also means "saintliness," and thus the contrast between the two, as Ibn 'Ajibah would say, is between the impermanence of the former, which has to do with the world, and the permanence of the latter, which has to do with the Hereafter.

125. "Beginnings" and "exteriors" tempt the ignorant man; "endings" and "interiors" force the intelligent man to be abstinent (Ibn 'Abbad). See Hikmah no. 85 for a similar thought.

126. Beneficial knowledge, in the thinking of Ibn 'Abbad, is knowledge of God, His Attributes, His Names, and knowledge of the acts of devotion and how to act before Him.

127. Both this Hikmah and the following one describe the type of knowledge that is beneficial to man, namely, the one accompanied by the fear of God. If there is no fear of God, then, as Ibn 'Ajibah would say, there is no good whatsoever in the knowledge, and eventually it works against man.

128. To understand this Hikmah aright, we have to know that, in Arabic, the term "humility" (tawadu') also means "lowliness." Thus, the individual strives to bring his "self" low, while the self, to paraphrase Ibn 'Ajibah, seeks loftiness. For the individual who has a certain spirituality, all things in the creation seem alike, whereas for those who have separative knowledge, all things have their hierarchic level. These last see themselves as having a distinction over and above the other things; they attribute lowliness to themselves. But the gnostics, who have a unitive knowledge, never attribute any distinction to themselves at all; they see things on a plane of equality and attribute neither lowliness nor loftiness to themselves.

129. The humble man, according to Ibn 'Abbad, is aware of his imperfections, and this awareness forces him to see himself as being below what he does.

130. This humility arises in the gnostics, explains Ibn 'Ajibah, because the contemplation of the Divinity implies the extinction of themselves.

131. He means by "believer" in this Hikmah the perfectly realized sage who sees every excellence in himself as proceeding from his Lord.

132. The "arenas of the soul" are all those interior struggles against the egocentric tendencies of the self that the contemplative must go through. It is this interior holy war that constitutes progress or movement in the Path, and not the traversing of some imaginary "distance" between man and God.

133. Man is a "microcosm," explains Ibn 'Abbad, and thus he contains in himself the mysteries or secrets of all created things, whether superior or inferior, spiritual or physical.

134. In commenting on this Hikmah, Ibn 'Ajibah speaks of the three fundamental degrees of reality, the *Mulk*, the *Malakut*, and the *Jabarut*, or the physical world, the psychic world, and the spiritual world, the last incorporating, not only the realities of a paradisiacal nature, but also the uncreated realities within God. In the process of realization, the gnostics perceive the *Mulk* as reabsorbed into the *Malakut*; and with greater refinement of perception, they see the *Malakut* as reabsorbed into the *Jabarut*, so that, in the final analysis, there is only the *Jabarut* that remains as the uniquely Real, the entire Cosmos having no hold whatsoever on the sages. Not so is the case of those individuals who have no unitive knowledge at all, but only separative knowledge—for them, illusion is at work and the *Mulk* veils them from God.

135. Human nature as such, according to Ibn 'Ajibah, is like the night; when the solar nature of God's Lordship (*rububiyyah*) rises within man, it is like the sun shining in the night, giving the appearance that the night, now become day, is itself luminous; but this is not so. Likewise is sanctity in man: The luminous nature of the Spirit can so overwhelm the individuality as to transform it totally into light; even so, that light is of transcendent origin and does not belong to man.

136. There is a distinction between the ecstatic contemplative (*majdhub*), who is drawn by celestial Attraction (*al-Jadhb*) from the very beginning, and the voyager (*salik*), the methodical initiate, who experiences from the outset the problems and difficulties of the Path; the former is "drunk," the latter is "sober." Ibn 'Ajibah explains that the saintly sages are of two kinds: those who begin with celestial Attraction without any effort on their part, then return to voyaging; and those who begin with voyaging (*suluk*), that is to say, the normative Path, then the celestial Attraction overtakes them. In this Hikmah, the phrase "created things" (*athar*) means the acts of God in the world; these multiple acts proceed from the divine Names and even point to them as to their origins. Likewise, the Names point to the Qualities, such as the Living, the Knowing, the Willing, and the like. They

147

in turn point to the divine Essence, from which everything proceeds. For the ecstatic, it is the divine Essence that appears first; then come the Qualities, and afterwards the Names, and finally the created things; so his way is a progressive descent (*tadallin* or *tanazzul*). The exact opposite is the course of the voyager: He starts with the created things; then come the Names, and afterwards the Qualities, and finally the divine Essence; so his way is a progressive ascension (*taraqqin*). Ibn 'Ajibah states that the one who has experienced the progressive ascension is more reliable in guiding others in the Path than the one who has experienced the opposite; the reason for this is that the *salik* has undergone the difficulties and hardships of the Path, while the *majdhub* has not. For most people in the Path, the initiatic voyaging (*suluk*) is normal, followed by celestial Attraction (*al-Jadhb*), whereas the case of the *majdhub* is rare. Ibn 'Ajibah also notes that the ascension is from the *Mulk* to the *Malakut* to the *Jabarut*, in the sense of a progressive reabsorption from the lowest level of reality to the highest. The "return" or "descent" is presumably the reverse: from the *Jabarut* to the *Malakut* to the *Mulk*.

137. The "invisible world" mentioned here is the Hereafter.

138. A similar idea is presented in Hikmah no. 72.

139. Ibn 'Abbad says that the methodical "voyager" (*salik*) is the one whose invocation precedes his illumination, whereas the "ecstatic" (*majdhub*) is the one whose illumination precedes his invocation.

140. That which appears externally comes from an internal source, as the author has already explained in Hikmah no. 28.

141. "Those with Him," as Ibn 'Ajibah says, are the angelic hosts.

142. These two kinds of meditation belong to two groups, according to Ibn 'Ajibah: The first meditation belongs to those still traveling toward God with the lights of orientation; the second belongs to those who are united with Him and have direct vision.

143. Qur'an 17:80.

144. The hidden associationism of dependence has to do with secondary causes, or creatures, as Ibn 'Ajibah points out: One depends on them and not on God as such.

145. This is a description of the perfect sage.

146. A'isha, one of the wives of the Prophet, was falsely accused of adultery. The phrase "when her innocence was revealed through the tongue of the Prophet" refers to the Qur'anic verses (24:11–20) dealing with the scandal and her exoneration.

147. Qur'an 31:14.

148. The "refreshment of the eye" (*qurrat al-'ayn*) is a classic expression in Arabic which also means "joy," "pleasure," "the eye's delight," etc.

149. Qur'an 10:58.

150. Qur'an 6:92.

151. Qur'an 6:44.

152. Qur'an 10:58.

153. Qur'an 6:92.

154. This is not a Qur'anic verse but merely a tradition the author is passing on to the reader.

155. One will recall here what the author has already mentioned about "essential indigence" in Hikmah no. 99.

156. Ibn 'Ajibah explains this discourse by saying that it alludes to the alternation of states coming over a servant, such as poverty and wealth, ignorance and knowledge, belief and disbelief, contraction and expansion, and so forth. Useless is it to repose in one state, for another one may suddenly arrive. Were he to cling to His "giving," it might disappear in an instant; were he to despair during trials, they too might vanish quickly.

157. God has attributed to Himself these qualities in the Qur'an; but He is gentle and kind "before" the appearance of creatures.

158. A person's virtues, according to Ahmad Zarruq, are strewn with defects, to begin with; hence, his vices cannot but be vices, being imperfections as such. Likewise, his interior realities, such as states or stations or ecstatic experiences, do not belong to him, given the intrinsic poverty of his nature; so his pretensions are really pretensions, with nothing substantial hidden in them.

159. The same theme is to be found in Hikmah no. 29.

160. Qur'an 66.8.

161. The Knowledge mentioned here, according to Ibn 'Abbad, is that which is given to the elect; the Name is the divine Name guarded from all alterities.

162. Those possessed by "attraction" (al-jadhb) are the lovers of God, for whom everything is easy, as Ibn 'Abbad explains.

163. "Contentment" is an attribute of God, and its root in God is His eternal nature, so there can be no cause for it in Him, says Ibn 'Abbad.

164. God's betaking Himself to His throne is a Qur'anic image; here it is a question of the All-Mercifulness and the throne, and this assumes the following verse from the Qur'an as a given: "The All-Merciful, who on the throne is established" (20:5). The "throne" is a cosmic principle that presides over the world from a central point of authority. The "throne" is also seen as an encompassing reality, enveloping the created world; but it is itself enveloped by the All-Mercifulness. To say that created things are annihilated by created things is to say that the universe is reabsorbed into its cosmic principle, the throne. The all-encompassing spheres of light, as Ibn

'Ajibah explains, are the lights of the divine Qualities, that obliterate all alterities, namely, the throne and all that it contains, so that all that remains is the radiance of the Divinity in Itself.

165. "He is the First and the Last and the Exterior and the Interior" (Qur'an 57:3).

Glossary

Sufi Technical Terms

'abd: the servant, the slave; the creature dependent on his Lord; the worshiper.

'abid (pl. **'ubbad**): the devotee; one who is occupied with the external acts of devotion. See also the *zahid* and the *'arif*.

aghyar: see *ghayr*.

'Alam al-Jabarut: the world of absolute Immensity or Sovereignty or Domination, which is that of the Spirit that transcends the psychic world; the highest of the three degrees of reality (*Jabarut, Malakut, Mulk*); the spiritual world of God and the angelic realities.

'Alam al-Malakut: the world of the Realm or the Dominion; the psychic world, intermediate between the *Jabarut* and the *Mulk*; the world of the soul.

'Alam al-Mulk: the world of the Kingdom; the physical or material world of existence; the third and lowest of the degrees of reality, coming after the *Malakut*.

'aql: the intellect or pure intelligence (the same as the *nous* of Plotinus); also the discursive reasoning, or reason, in contrast to the transcendent intellect; the same as *basirah*.

'arif (pl. **'arifun**): the gnostic, in contrast to the *'abid* and the *zahid*; he who has gnosis (*ma'rifah*) of God, which implies that he is a saintly sage.

asbab: see *sabab*.

asrar: see *sirr*.

athar: trace, created thing, creature, being; in the plural it denotes multiplicity; the manifestation of the divine Qualities in the world.

'ayn al-basirah: the eye of the intellect; the intermediate stage in the process of intellection, when the intellective eye perceives the Real but is not yet reabsorbed in it; after *shu'a' al-basirah* and before *Haqq al-basirah*; corresponds to *'ayn al-yaqin*.

'ayn al-qalb: the eye of the heart; the intellect (*'aql*) as the eye of intellective vision of the Real in the heart (to be distinguished from the *'aql* as reason, situated in the brain or its subtle counterpart); the same as *basirah*.

'ayn al-yaqin: the eye of certitude, the vision of certitude; the state resulting from illumination; the second of the three degrees of knowledge after *'ilm al-yaqin* and before *Haqq al-yaqin*.

GLOSSARY

baqa': subsistence, permanence; the state of one who has been reintegrated in the Spirit and has unitive knowledge of the Absolute; the opposite of *fana'*.

basirah: inner vision; the faculty of the intellect (*'aql*); clear vision; the eye of the heart (*'ayn al-qalb*).

bast: expansion in a spiritual sense, though it does have psychological repercussions; it is positive and attended with external signs of joy and gladness and bliss; the opposite of *qabd*.

batin: the interior, the esoteric; as al-Batin, "the Interior," it is one of the ninety-nine Names of *Allah*; the opposite of *zahir*.

bu'd: remoteness, distance from God; opposite of *qurb*.

dhat: the essence of something; the self-subsistent essence of anything, in contrast to the *sifah*, or attribute or quality; as *adh-Dhat*, it is the Essence of God, absolutely self-subsistent.

dhawq: taste, intuition.

dhikr: remembering, remembrance of God; the invocation of one of the Names of *Allah*.

dhikru 'llah: the invocation of God; the remembrance of God in a general fashion; the invocation of a divine Name, which is the fundamental method of spiritual concentration in Sufism.

fana': extinction, evanescence; the extinction of all that blocks the individual from union with God; the opposite of *baqa'*.

faqir (pl. fuqara'): poor man; a seeker who has the quality of poverty in a spiritual sense (*faqr*); an adherent to the Sufi Path, an initiate.

faqr: spiritual poverty, the fundamental virtue in Sufism; detachment of the Spirit from all multiplicity within the mind.

fikrah: meditation, reflective thinking about the divine Attributes or Qualities.

ghayr (pl. aghyar): the other; alterity; the other-than-God (*al-ghayr*).

hal (pl. ahwal): spiritual state; a passing state, opposed to *maqam*.

haqiqah: esoteric truth; inner reality; al-Haqiqah is the divine Reality, source of the *tariqah* and *shari'ah*.

haqq: right, duty; al-Haqq is the Truth, the Real, God, and is opposed to *Khalq*.

Haqq al-basirah: the Truth of the intellect; the third and final perception of the Real after *shu'a' al-basirah* and *'ayn al-basirah*; corresponds to *Haqq al-yaqin*; all duality disappears at this level of consciousness.

GLOSSARY

Haqq al-yaqin: the Truth of certitude; the third and final degree of certitude with regard to the Absolute; corresponds to *Haqq al-basirah*; comes after *'ayn al-yaqin*.

himmah (pl. himam): decisive force, spiritual aspiration, fervor.

hubut: as *al-Hubut*, the Fall of mankind from the Garden of Eden.

Ibn al-Waqt: the son of the instant, or moment; the Sufi insofar as he lives in the present, not in the past or in the future.

idhn: permission, authority to guide others in the Path.

ihsan: spiritual virtue; the third of the three stations or conditions of the Islamic faith: *islam*, *iman*, and *ihsan*.

'ilm al-yaqin: the science of certitude; the first and most elementary degree of certitude, resulting from proof and demonstration, the theoretical teachings of Sufism, and consequently the beginning of the Path; followed by *'ayn al-yaqin*.

iman: faith; faith in the Divinity, but in Sufism this is considered the second of the three stations of Islam, not the first as in exoteric Islam: *islam*, *iman*, and *ihsan*.

islam: submission to the divine Will, especially as it manifested itself in the ritual Law; in Sufism, the first of the three stations of Islam, followed by *iman* and *ihsan*.

Jabarut: see *'Alam al-Jabarut*.

jadhb: attraction, in a spiritual sense; the celestial Attraction exerted on those following the Path, especially on the *majdhub*; the term has connotations of grace and blessings of a supernatural nature.

Khalq: as *al-Khalq*, the Creation, or the entire Universe insofar as it is distinguished from *al-Haqq*, the Truth, or the uncreated Real, the ontological Principle of the Creation; the two are often juxtaposed as Absolute and relative.

majdhub: the ecstatic contemplative, the one drawn upward by celestial attraction without any effort on his part; often referred to as spiritually intoxicated, in contrast to the *salik*.

Malakut: see *'Alam al-Malakut*.

maqam (pl. maqamat): station; the spiritual station of a permanent nature; the opposite of *hal*.

ma'rifah: gnosis, or direct knowledge of God; the goal of the Sufi Path; the obtainment of gnosis implies saintliness and wisdom; often contrasted with the ascetical and devotional life; he who has *ma'rifah* is an *'arif*.

Mulk: see *'Alam al-Mulk*.

GLOSSARY

mutajarrid: the recluse, the contemplative who withdraws from society and leads a life of mendicancy. (He lives in a state of *tajrid.*)

mutasabbib: the Sufi adherent who lives in the midst of society and gains his own livelihood (*sabab*, pl. *asbab*).

nafs (pl. **nufus**): the soul, the ego, the psyche, the subtle reality of the individual; corresponds to the *Malakut* among the degrees of reality.

niyyah: the intention, said to be situated in the heart.

nur (pl. **anwar**): light, either physical or psychic or spiritual; *an-Nur* is the divine Light, uncreated in itself but with cosmic manifestations that are created but spiritual.

qabd: contraction, in a spiritual sense, not psychic or psychological; it has psychological reflections in sadness or sorrow; the opposite of *bast*.

qalb: the heart; the faculty of contemplative vision; corresponds to the physical heart in its centrality; it can become the receptacle of passion, sentiments, ignorance, and vices, or the receptacle of luminous virtues and knowledge, according to case.

qurb: nearness to God; the opposite of *bu'd*.

rububiyyah: *ar-Rububiyyah* is the quality or nature of God as Lord of the Universe, both in an immanent and transcendent sense; the Lordship or Lordliness of God, in contrast with the servant's *'ubudiyyah*.

ruh (pl. **arwah**): the vital spirit, intermediary between body and soul; the Spirit, beyond the soul or the psyche; the uncreated Spirit or the created Spirit; it is the innermost being or secret (*sirr*), corresponding to the *Jabarut*.

sabab (pl. **asbab**): cause, secondary cause; means of livelihood; profession, trade.

sahw: sobriety or soberness in a spiritual sense; a characteristic of the *salik* but not of the *majdhub*.

salik: the voyager in the Path; he who follows the Path methodically, starting with creatures and experiencing difficulties and hardships in the beginning; characterized by sobriety and contrasted with the *majdhub*.

shari'ah: the sacred Law of Islam, based on the Qur'an and the Sunnah of the Prophet and leading to salvation in a posthumous state; the Law binding on all Muslims; the first stage in the way of realization, followed by the *tariqah*, which leads to the *Haqiqah*.

shaykh: spiritual master or guide in the Sufi Path who has permission or authority to teach others the way of realization.

155

shirk: the cardinal sin of associationism; paganism or polytheism; the association of something alongside of the One, who is *Allah*; the opposite of *tawhid*.

shu'a' al-basirah: the ray of light of the intellect; the first stage in the process of intellection, when the intellective eye (i.e., the eye of the heart, or *'ayn al-qalb*) becomes aware of the Real through reflected or diffused light, not through actual direct vision; corresponds to *'ilm al-yaqin*, or the theoretical degree of certitude.

sifah (pl. sifat): quality, attribute, either of the individual or of God, and that is not self-subsistent, in contrast to an essence (*dhat*).

sirr (pl. asrar): secret, mystery; the innermost center of consciousness in man, which emerges from the *Jabarut*; the most luminous point in man; when reabsorbed into the Real it is the Self, or the divine Immanence.

sirr al-khususiyyah: the mystery or secret of election; the inner reality of sanctity; when used alone, *khususiyyah* refers to the particular charismatic attributes of a seeker in the Path.

sukr: inebriety, drunkenness in a spiritual sense; a characteristic of the *majdhub* but not of the *salik*; the opposite of *sahw*.

suluk: methodical voyaging in the Path, starting with creatures and moving up to the uncreated realities in God.

tadbir: self-direction, self-willing; God's direction or planning; the *tadbir* can be either good or bad, depending on whether it conforms to God's will or not.

tajrid: isolation for the purpose of contemplation; isolation as opposed to being in the world to gain a living; the opposite of *sabab*.

tanazzul: descent or redescent from the divine Reality; the descent of the *majdhub* from the Essence to the Qualities to the Names to the created forms; the opposite of *taraqqin*.

taraqqin: ascension or ascent; the ascent of the *salik* from the created forms to the Names to the Qualities to the divine Essence; the opposite of *tanazzul*.

tariqah: spiritual Path, or Sufism; the second term in the ternary *shari'ah, tariqah, Haqiqah*.

tawhid: the affirmation of the Oneness of *Allah*, the rejection of polytheism or associationism; the affirmation that there is but one Absolute.

'ubbad: see *'abid*.

'ubudiyyah: servanthood; the state of obedience; it consists in fulfilling the rights due to God as Lord or as having Lordship (*rububiyyah*); man's servanthood is the opposite of the Lordship of God.

GLOSSARY

wahm: opinion, conjecture, suspicion; deluded imagination; illusion; the conjectural faculty.

waqt: the moment, the instant; the "now" that reflects Eternity, the non-temporal present, outside the process of past or future time.

warid (pl. *waridat*): inspiration, in the sense of a luminous insight.

wird (pl. *awrad*): a litany to be recited.

zahid (pl. *zuhhad*): ascetic, or one who renounces the world; he who is occupied with asceticism; contrasted with the *'abid* and the *'arif*.

zahir: the exterior, the exoteric; as *az-Zahir*, "the Exterior," it is one of the ninety-nine Names of *Allah*; the opposite of *batin*.

zuhhad: see *zahid*.

Bibliography

General works on Sufism

Attar, Farid ad-Din. *Muslim Saints and Mystics*. Translated from the Persian by A. J. Arberry, London, 1966.

Austin, R.W. *Sufis of Andalucia*. Translated from the Arabic of Ibn al-'Arabi, Los Angeles, 1972.

Burckhardt, Titus. *An Introduction to Sufi Doctrine*. Wellingborough, England, 1976.

Corbin, Henry. *Creative Imagination in the Sufism of Ibn 'Arabi*. Translated from the French by Ralph Manheim, Princeton, 1969.

Hujwiri. *Kashf al-mahjub*. Translated from the Persian work of the same title by R. A. Nicholson, London, 1911.

Ibn al-'Arabi. *The Wisdom of the Prophets*. Translated from the French of Titus Burckhardt by Angela Culme-Seymour, Aldsworth, England, 1975.

Ibn al-'Arif. *Mahasin al-majalis*. Arabic text, translation into French, and commentary by Asin Palacios, Paris, 1933.

Jami. *Lawa'ih*. Translated from Persian by E. H. Whinfield and M. M. Kazvini, London, 1906.

Jili, 'Abd al-Karim. *De l'Homme universel*. Extracts from *al-Insan al-Kamil* by Jili, translated into French from the Arabic by Titus Burckhardt, Lyons, 1955.

Kalabadhi, Muhammad. *The Doctrine of the Sufis*. Translated from the Arabic by A. J. Arberry, New York, 1966.

Lings, Martin. *A Sufi Saint of the Twentieth Century: Shaikh Ahmad al-'Alawi*. Los Angeles, 1973.

Massignon, Louis. *Essai sur les origines du lexique technique de la mystique musulmane*. Rev. ed. Paris, 1968.

Mawlay al-'Arabi ad-Darqawi. *Letters of a Sufi Master*. Translated from the Arabic by Titus Burckhardt, London, 1969.

Michon, Jean-Louis. *Le Soufi marocain Ahmad ibn Ajiba et son Mi'raj*. Paris, 1973.

Molé, Marijan. *Les mystiques musulmans*. Paris, 1965.

Nasr, S.H. *Sufi Essays*. New York, 1977.

———. *Three Muslim Sages*. Cambridge, Mass., 1964.

Nicholson, R. A. *The Mystics of Islam*. London, 1963.

BIBLIOGRAPHY

_____ . *Studies in Islamic Mysticism*. Cambridge, 1921.

Nwyia, Paul. *Ibn 'Ata' Allah et la naissance de la confrerie sadilite*. Beirut, 1972.

Padwick, Constance. *Muslim Devotions: A Study of Prayer-Manuals in Common Use*. London, 1961.

Rinn, L. *Marabouts et Khouans*. Algiers, 1884.

Ritter, H. *Das Meer der Seele: Mensch, Welt und Gott in den Geschichten des Fariduddin 'Attar*. Leiden, 1955.

Schaya, Leo. *La Doctrine soufique de l'Unité*. Paris, 1962.

Schimmel, Annemarie. *The Mystical Dimensions of Islam*. Chapel Hill, N.C., 1975.

Schuon, Frithjof. *Islam and the Perennial Philosophy*. London, 1976.

────. *Understanding Islam*. London, 1963.

────. *The Transcendent Unity of Religions*. Rev. ed. New York, 1975.

Siraj ad-Din, Abu Bakr. *The Book of Certainty*. New York, 1970.

Stoddart, William. *Sufism: The Mystical Doctrines and Methods of Islam*. London, 1976.

Khwaja 'Abdullah Ansari

Intimate Conversations

(Munajat)

Introduction and Translation

by

W. M. Thackston, Jr.

Foreword

Koranic commentator, collector, transmitter of Prophetic reports (*hadith*), indefatigable defender of the stern Hanbalite school of literal interpetation of Islamic law and custom, 'Abdullah Ansari (1006–1089), known as the Pir of Herat, is one of the major early figures in the development of Persian mystical literature.

Famed in the history of Sufism for his *Tabaqat al-sufiyya*, a Persian translation of and elaboration on Sulami's work on the lives and sayings of prominent Sufis, Ansari is chiefly renowned among Persian-speaking people for his *Munajat*, or intimate conversations with God, a collection of simple, flowing, sometimes rhymed Persian sentences culled posthumously by his disciples from his larger works. In this small collection, which has served long generations of the spiritually inclined as a devotional handbook, Ansari speaks of his love and longing for his Creator as well as of his frustration and anguish in abject, human frailty vis-à-vis God's omnipotence.

The present work is a selected translation of the corpus of intimate conversations with God traditionally attributed to Khwaja 'Abdullah Ansari.

Introduction

The old province of Khurasan, which included much of modern Iran and today's Afghanistan and stretched northward to the Oxus, played a prominent role throughout Islamic history. One of the centers of this vast province was Herat, where Alexander the Great is known to have built a city called Alexandria in Aria. An important seat of learning during the middle period of Islamic civilization, second only in cultural and scholarly importance to Nishapur, Herat was to Abu-Isma'il 'Abdullah Ansari (1006–1089) home for all but brief portions of his life. Born in May in the ancient citadel of Herat, Quhandiz, Ansari, known as Khwaja 'Abdullah and as the Pir of Herat, says of himself, "I am 'vernal,' for I was born in the spring. I love spring very much. The Sun was in the seventeenth degree of Taurus when I was born, and every time it reaches that point again I complete another year. It is the middle of spring, the season of flowers and herbs."[1]

Descended from an Arab who had settled in Herat with the conquering armies of Islam in the 7th century,[2] Khwaja 'Abdullah inherited a tendency toward Sufism, the "inner" or spiritual aspect of Islam, from his father, Aub-Mansur Muhammad, who had been trained in the way of abstinence and renunciation of worldly affairs by an ascetic in Balkh. Having returned to his native Herat, where he opened a shop in the bazaar, married and produced children, Aub-Mansur was at last overcome by nostalgia for his former life and, abandoning his young family, sought again the ascetic coterie around the Sharif Hamza 'Aqili in Balkh, where he remained until his death in 1039.[3]

The young 'Abdullah was given a traditional education and training in the Islamic sciences of *hadith* (reports on the custom and usage of the Prophet and of the first generation of Muslims), Koranic reading, and interpretation and Islamic jurisprudence (*fiqh*). In search of further scholarly training, Ansari traveled to Nishapur, then the center of learning in the eastern realm of Islam, where he studied law, *hadith*, Arabic grammar, and Koran with illustrious masters of these branches of learning.

Of all those whom he met and with whom he studied, there were two men who made lasting impressions on the young scholar from Herat. One was Shaykh Abu-'Abdullah Taqi, from whom he acquired his attachment to Hanbalite doctrine. "He was my master and teacher in the Hanbalite creed," said Ansari. "Had I never seen him, I would never have come to know the belief of the Hanbalites."[4] The second was an illiterate villager, Abu'l-Hasan Kharaqani.

Ansari's Hanbalite doctrinal stand set him squarely at odds with the then dominant school of theological interpretation, scholastic Ash'arism. Although at its outset Ash'arism had represented a step toward reliance on a literal interpretation of the revealed word as final authority and away from the rational argumentation of the practitioners of the *kalam*, the Islamic theological dialectic, in the course of time Ash'arism had succumbed to the rational methodology of its original opponents. The extreme rationalists, giving more weight to logical reasoning than to the letter of revelation, were accused by their Ash'arite opponents of stripping God of all attributes except His unknowable Essence. The Ash'arites had restored the attributes to God's Essence but qualified them by saying that they were in no fashion similar to the corresponding human attributes. Anthropomorphic allusions in the Koran, such as references to God's "hand" and "face," extreme rationalists took as pure metaphor; the Ash'arites held them to be real attributes, but again not corporeal. Nonetheless, the Ash'arites, in admitting rational methods, had developed by the 11th century into thoroughly intellectualistic theologians.[5]

INTRODUCTION

Dead set against allowing any such "heretical innovation" into their camp, the Hanbalites clung to the letter of the Koran and Sunna (the practice of the early community as reported in *hadith*) and rejected vehemently any rational deliberations on theological concerns. For them the literal meaning of the divine word of the Koran and the utterances of the Prophet was the final authority on matters theological. While rationalists might explain away anthropomorphic allusions in the Koran to, for example, God's "hand" by saying that it was to be taken metaphorically for His power or that it was a quality and not a corporeal member, the Hanbalites maintained that when God had said "hand" in His Koran, He meant a corporeal hand and nothing else. Their strictly literal interpretation thus laid the Hanbalites open to charges of anthropomorphism and even idolatry by the politically more powerful Ash'arites of the time. And a ferociously tenacious Hanbalite—"bigoted" and "fanatic" said some—like 'Abdullah Ansari could be, and was, made to suffer for his beliefs by being barred from teaching and even sent into exile. Due to the calumny of his rationalist enemies, Ansari was summoned before the Ghaznavid Sultan Mas'ud in 1039 and questioned on his anthropomorphic interpretations. During this interview he not only exonerated himself but was dismissed by the Sultan with honors. Later, in 1043, he was so threatened with hostility from the opposing camp that he was forced to quit Herat for a period of two years. In 1066 he was actually exiled formally by an edict from the Grand Vizier of the Seljuq Empire, Nizam al-Mulk; this exile was of short duration, however, and he was back in Herat within the year. Finally, after a change of attitude regarding dogma on the part of the central authorities, Khwaja 'Abdullah was invested with a robe of honor and the title Shaykh al-Islam by the Caliph al-Qa'im bi-Amrillah in 1070. Although blind in his old age, Ansari remained an active teacher of Islamic sciences, maintaining his animosity toward the rationalist schools of thought, and master to his band of devoted disciples until his death in 1089. His tomb at Gazargah, just outside of Herat, continues to this day to be one of the most venerated sites in the Muslim world.

Ceaseless in his efforts on behalf of Hanbalism, Ansari wrote several books in which he attacked the rationalists and their method. His largest polemical work is *Dhamm al-Kalam wa-ahlih* [The Shame of the Theological Dialectic and of Those Who Practice It], in which he tries to prove that the Prophet condemned in advance the machinations of the theologians in their subtle discourses, discussions, interpretation of the Koran independent of Sunna, opposition of reason to *hadith*, exercise of personal initiative to fathom religion, exegesis that attempted to go beyond the literal sense, and attention accorded to what Christians and Jews had to say. In the second part of this book he shows that all the religious authorities in Islam have rejected these same machinations; their statements he collects and groups according to the epoch in which the authors lived.[6] In his *Kitab al-arba'in fi dala'il al-tawhid* Book of Forty in Proof of Divine Unity, most likely written between 1064 and 1070, he collects forty *hadiths* in order to prove the reality of God's corporeal attributes.[7] He is also known to have written a number of pamphlets debunking the theological claims of several groups considered by him to be heretical innovators.[8]

At variance with the latitudinarian attitude of many later Sufis but in keeping with the precepts of many of the masters of spirituality, Ansari's strict Hanbalite adherence to the letter of Islamic law and custom and fastidious attention to ritual detail in no way excluded, and in many ways actually complemented, the inner, or spiritual, path of Islam known as Sufism. By meditating on the words of the Koran and the Custom of the Prophet, the Sufis discovered within themselves a personal deity with whom they could have direct and immediate contact through a gnosis, or knowledge, that depended in no way on the rational function of the intellect but rather on the intuitive function of the heart.[9] Throughout the *Munajat* the reader will find allusions to and expansions of the Arabic dictum, *man 'arafa nafsahu fa-qad 'arafa rabbahu* ["Who knows himself, knows his Lord," echoing the ancient Delphic gnothi s'auton ["Know thyself!"].

In his spiritual life, aside from his father's ascetic influence, Ansari's greatest inspiration was a simple, unlettered villager filled with mystical fervor, Abu'l-Hasan Kharaqani, whose disciple Ansari always considered himself. "Had I never met Kharaqani," says Khwaja 'Abdullah, "I would never have known the Divine Reality."[10] From Kharaqani he learned that being a Sufi does not consist of outward appearance, as Kharaqani said when asked what a Sufi was: "One does not become a Sufi by virtue of one's patched frock and prayer-mat; one does not become a Sufi by adopting the customs and manners of the Sufis; a Sufi is that which is not!"[11] To be a Sufi for Kharaqani meant to be totally detached and liberated from the world and all it contains, to be dependent on and desirous of nothing: "A Sufi is a day that has no need of the sun, a night that has no need of the moon and stars, a 'not-being' that has no need of 'being.' "[12] Following Kharaqani, Khwaja 'Abdullah defines being a dervish, or Sufi, as being "something that neither harms the soles of the feet nor leaves a trail of dust behind," by which he means that the Sufi perfects himself through absolute spiritual poverty, by reducing himself through humility until he reaches the lowliness of the dust, which, unlike stones and thorns that reach up to injure the feet of those who tread on them, is passively trampled on by the world; in divesting oneself of all worldly attachments and wants, until he becomes a "stranger to kith and kin," the Sufi "abstracts" himself from worldly possessions to the point that he is encumbered by no holdings and leaves not even a "trail of dust" behind himself.

Well aware of the pitfall of pride in one's accomplishments on the Sufi path, Khwaja 'Abdullah is glad for his human frailty and awareness of his disobedience to God's law, for it is that very awareness that brings him to his knees in repentance. The reader of the *Munajat* will notice that the two concepts of "obedience" (*ta'at*) and "disobedience" (*ma'siyat*) are stressed throughout. In Islam, the Koran is God's Word, in which His eternal Law for mankind was revealed to the Prophet Muhammad: The precepts enjoined therein are binding upon all who profess Islam (which means "submission" to God's will and command). A Muslim (in Arabic the word means "one who submits") therefore freely subjugates his own will to God's and chooses to obey His commands as a faithful servant. The True Way then lies in obedience to God, and deviation from that Path consists of disobedience to, or violation of, God's law. Whereas the Islamic schools of legal thought were generally of the opinion that men were to be held to account for external breaches of the divinely legislated code (*shari'a*), the Sufis, who trod the inward "path of the heart," felt that they would be called to reckoning for any "disobedience" in thought, word, or deed.

Leaving aside his polemic in the *Munajat*, Ansari chides the ascetics for being merely "wage-earners of heaven." In their dry abstinence, ascetics deprive themselves of the pleasures of this world in hope of gaining much the same pleasures as a reward, or wage, in the next world. What they lack is the love and yearning for God that mark the true Sufi. Devoid of both fear of hell-fire and anticipation of heavenly reward without the *visio Dei*, the true Sufi labors purely for God's sake, for the delight of serving Him without thought for compensation either now or in the Hereafter.

In the field of mysticism, Ansari's works that survive include his famous *Tabaqat al-sufiyya*, [13] a translation into Herati Persian in expanded format of Sulami's (d. 1021) *Tabaqat al-sufiyyin*, a collection of brief biographical notices and sayings of prominent Sufis. This work, put together as a volume by one or more of the Khwaja's disciples who had access to his notes, was one of the major sources for 'Abd al-Rahman Jami (1414–

1492) in his authoritative *Nafahat al-uns*. In the teachings, comments on his predecessors, development of doctrinal points, poetry, and *munajats* it contains, this rambling opus gives a vivid picture of Ansari the master Sufi.

His commentary on the Koran was unfortunately never finished; but as it forms the basis of *Kashf al-asrar wa-'uddat al-abrar*,[14] begun in 1126 by Rashid al-Din Ahmad Maybudi, one can see Ansari's thought and method of mystical Koranic interpretation at work.

His other, smaller works are mainly of the nature of handbooks of Sufism and treatises on mystical states and stages. *Sad maydan*,[15] Ansari's first work, centers almost exclusively on love for God and shows the development of his thought on the spiritual Path to 1056. *Manazil al-sa'irin*,[16] one of Khawaja 'Abdullah's most widely circulated works, treats in a more mature fashion the mystical progression toward unity with the Divine. Dictated to his disciples Abu'l-Waqt Sijzi, 'Abd al-Malik Karukhi, and Muhammad Saydalani, this often commented-on book was completed in the year 475 of the Hegira (A.D. 1082–1083). In *'Ilal al-maqamat*,[17] an expansion on one aspect dealt with in the *Manazil*, the Khwaja expounds on the dangers involved in each of the mystical "stages" (*maqamat*). *Kanz al-salikin*,[18] a vademecum for the aspirant Sufi, is also known as the pseudo-*Manazil*. *al-Mukhtasar fi adab al-sufiyya*[19] is a breviarium on the correct comportment of a Sufi.

The *Nasihatnama-i vazir*, or *Nasiha-i Nizam al-Mulk*,[20] falls into the genre of sage counsel, this one addressed to the Grand Vizier of the Seljuqs, Nizam al-Mulk.

Of all of Khwaja 'Abdullah Ansari's works, the one that has remained the most popular through the centuries and the one that has exercised the most profound influence on Persian stylistics is the *Munajat*.[21] The word *munajat* is derived from the Arabic verb, *naja*, which means "to have an intimate conversation with someone." The sentences that are contained in the *Munajat* form an intensely personal and familiar monologue addressed to God. Each sentence beings with the Arabic vocative *ilahi* ("my God"), a device used by Kharaqani in many of his recorded sayings and one that Ansari may have adopted from his spiritual master.[22] The *Munajat* was not composed by Ansari as a separate work; the collection was made by his students and disciples, who culled his other works, mainly the *Tabaqat*, and extracted sentences of the *munajat* type to form a "sampler" of Ansari's rapport with God. Over the centuries, in the words of Ansari's modern editor, the *Munajat* has often changed its complexion and has also "snowballed."[23] Indeed, to judge by content alone without regard to style, some of the book as it is now known cannot be ascribed to Khwaja 'Abdullah, betraying as it does elements common to later Sufistic thought. The language in which Ansari wrote and dictated, as we know from the oldest surviving manuscripts of his corpus, was the dialect form of Persian current in 11th-century Herat.[24] The dialectal peculiarities, however, have been normalized by successive copyists and redactors, who, typical of premodern litterateurs in the Perso-Arabic tradition, did not hesitate to make "corrections" and "amendments," not to speak of additions, in accordance with their own personal taste. The result is a collection of prose sentences, characteristically rhymed, the ascription of which to the Pir of Herat rests on a certain historical basis but to which later accretions have adhered.[25] What the modern collection does share with the original core of the work is the intimate, personal, and conversational tenor the speaker adopts in addressing God. Couched in sometimes humble, sometimes reproachful language, the speaker assumes the familiar position vis-à-vis God that a faithful servant of long tenure might assume in speaking to his master. Ansari is aware that his obligation to God is so overwhelming that he is incapable of even beginning to utter thanks. At the same time he is not beyond a good-natured chide at God for having put mankind into such an awkward position, ontologically speaking.

The format given the *Munajat* by Ansari's disciples consists of isolated prose sentences in no particular order and with no particular relation one to the other, among which are scattered lines of his poetry and an occasional quatrain. As this mixture of prose and poetry was adopted by Sa'di of Shiraz in his *Gulistan*, one of the undisputed masterpieces of Persian literature, it is interesting to speculate that he may have taken Ansari's *Munajat* as a model.[26] As a genre, the *munajat* gained in popularity after Ansari and even became an essential part of the Persian epic romance, taking its place between the sections on God's unity and on the Prophet.

Although we can render, however imperfectly, the sense of the *Munajat* into English, the peculiar Persian formal expression is lost to us. Ansari's sentences appear to be the essence of stylistic simplicity, yet masked by the brevity and conciseness of expression is a considerable amount of subtle rhetorical play. The parallelism and internal rhyme characteristic of so many of the prose sentences are devices impossible to recapture in translation. Extensive use is made of the rhetorical device known as *tarsi*, where the sequence of vowels in two or more parallel lines is exactly the same, with only the consonants varying, as in

ilāhī,
> *ḥāẓír-ī   che jūyam?*
> *nāẓír-ī   che gūyam?*

The use of internal rhyme at pausal points, a devise known as *saj'*, encountered throughout the Koran and common in Arabic and Persian literary style, gives these sentences an extraordinary rhythmical fluidity and cadences, as in

ilāhī,
farmūdī *karīm-am* *umīd* *bar ān* *tamām-ast*
va-chongúftī *rahīm-am* *naumīdī* *bar mā* *harām-ast*

Here the two sets of rhymes are held more tightly together by
the same final rhyme-consonant, *-m* (*-īm-/-ām-//-īm-/-ām-*).
The flow of the line is often punctuated by the parallel juxtaposition of antonyms, as in the above, *umīd* ("hope") and
naumıdı ("hopelessness").

Where the *tarsi'* structure is broken, Ansari often em-
ploys the repetition of a like syllable, as in

ilāhī
chon dar to *nigaram, az jumla-i tājdārān-am-o tāj bar sar*
chon dar khwad nigaram, az jumla-i khāksārān-am-o khāk bar sar

Frequent use is also made of the script-pun, where two words
or compounds are spelled alike in Persian but differ by an
extra, unwritten morphological vowel, as *taj-dar* ("crowned")
and *taj-i-dar* ("crown of the gallows"), which occurs elsewhere
("Hallaj said . . . ") . The use of near homonyms, such as *ta'at*
("obedience") and *taqat* ("endurance"), and of pseudo-
etymology, where two words appear to be derived from the
same root but are actually not, as *hajat* ("need") and *hujjat*
("proof, defense"), is responsible for a juxtaposition of concepts
that in translation often appears peculiar; but this is true of
much of Persian artful prose and certainly of poetry.

The first two parts of *Munajat* were translated from the
Teheran lithograph of 1358 H. lunar/1318 H. solar (A.D.
1940). The third section, the "Song of the Dervish," was translated from the final pages of the Mir 'Imad calligraphic repro-
duction (Teheran, 1333 [= *1955*]).

INTRODUCTION

A Note on the Text of the Munajat

There is as yet no modern scholarly edition of Khwaja Abdullah's *Munajat*. There is not even a standardized text. Over the centuries the collection known to us as the *Munajat* of the Pir of Herat has been amended and "corrected" by well-meaning copyists. It has been added to and subtracted from by litterateurs who, in the best Persian literary tradition, thought they were improving upon the original; and—the modern reader must in some cases admit—they did indeed make improvements upon the text as they found it. If we were to edit out all that is obviously (and subtlely) not the words of Khwaja Abdullah, we would lose much of value and beauty. The text has stood as it is, without significant change, for a number of centuries now; and we have a collection that has inspired an untold number of individuals. It is this version we wish to present, however meagrely, to the modern reader of English.

Versions of the Munajat

It is probably safe to say that no two printed versions of the *Munajat* agree with regard to the material included. Some are significantly longer; others markedly whittled-down. The most inclusive version the translator has seen is the Teheran lithograph, which seems to comprise many sentences taken from Ansari's corpus at large. As the sentences are grouped there, the first two sections comprise the bulk of material common to most generally available versions of the work. The smaller edition brought out in facsimile by the Bibliophile Society at Teheran contains very little not found in the first two sections of the lithograph. The last section of the facsimile (here called "The Song of the Dervish") is a grouping of sentences found throughout the third and fourth sections of the lithograph.

178

INTRODUCTION

Of the three groupings chosen for translation (the first two of the Teheran lithograph and the last of the facsimile) not more than ten sentences were deleted from the translation. A sentence was omitted from translation only when the sense was so subordinated to a linguistic play or rhyme that meaningful translation was deemed impossible.

Khwaja 'Abdullah Ansari

Intimate Conversations with God

(Munajat)

In the agony suffered for you,
the wounded find the scent of balm:
The memory of you consoles the souls of lovers.
Thousands in every corner, seeking a glimpse of you,
cry out like Moses, "Lord, show me yourself!"[1]
I see thousands of lovers lost in a desert of grief,
wandering aimlessly and saying hopefully,
"O God! O God!"
I see breasts scorched by the burning separation from you;
I see eyes weeping in love's agony.
Dancing down the lane of blame and censure,
your lovers cry out, "Poverty is my source of pride!"[2]
Pir-i Ansar[3] has quaffed the wine of longing:
Like Majnun[4] he wanders drunk and perplexed
through the world.

1

O God,
You are merciful in your might,
You are glorious in your beauty.
You are not needful of space,
You require not time.
No one resembles you;
You resemble no one.
It is evident that you are in the soul—
Nay, rather the soul lives by something which you are.

O God,
You subsist through your own grace.
Only you are capable of rendering thanks to yourself.
You are close to the knowledge of those who know you,
But you are far from what we imagine you to be.

O God,
To praise you for your greatness is a means to happiness,
But to open our mouths in thanks for your beneficence
raises us to the level of pride.

O God,
When you brand a heart with your love,
You scatter its heap of being to the winds of nonexistence.

O God,
Whosoever comes to know you
And raises the banner of your love
Will cast off all that is other than you.

KHWAJA 'ABDULLAH ANSARI

What use has he of his soul who has known you?
What use has he of offspring and family?
When you drive one mad,
You give him both this world and the next:
What use has the madman for this world or the next?

O God,
When I look upon you,
I see myself a king among kings,
A crown on my head.
When I look upon myself,
I see myself among the humble,
Dust on my head.[5]

O God,
I have wasted my life
And sone injustice to my body.

O God,
In our head we have intoxication by you,
In our heart we have your mysteries,
On our tongue we have your poetry.

O God,
If we speak, we speak praise of you.
If we seek, we seek your pleasure.

O God,
Of this world and the next I have chosen to love you:
I have put on coarse garments
And I have forsaken my well-being.

O God,
Everyone is a pauper in what he has not;
But I, in what I have.

O God,
Even though I am not very obedient,
Still I have no one but you.

O God,
There is no limit to your grace.
There is no tongue capable of uttering thanks to you.

O God,
Ask us not what we have produced
that we should not be perplexed!
Ask us not what we have done
that we should not be disgraced!

O God,
Seek not from us obedience to you,[6]
for we are not capable.
Speak not of our worthiness of you,
for we are too ashamed.

O God,
Outwardly I am disheveled
and inwardly I am in ruins.
My breast is aflame
and my eyes atear.
At times I burn in the fire of my breast
and at times I drown in my tears.

O God,
From your victim flows no blood.
From one burned by you rises no smoke.
He who is killed by you is happy to be killed.
He who is burned by you is glad to be burned.

KHWAJA 'ABDULLAH ANSARI

O God,
You commanded us to obey you
and then prevented us from doing so.
You forbade us to disobey you
and then made us disobedient.
You who are slow to anger and swift to make amends,
You have raised the banner of imperfection over our heads.

O God,
You summon us down a path in which are pitfalls.
If I fall into a pit, what fault is it of my companions?

O God,
What is it to have mercy on the obedient?
What is the value of mercy when it extends to everyone?

O God,
If Satan taught man evil,
who provided him with the wheat?[7]

O God,
You are ever-present.
Why then should I search?
You are ever-mindful.
What then should I say?

O God,
You see and know:
You are able to bring everything to fruition.

O God,
You do whatever you wish.
What then do you desire of this poor wretch?

O God,
When the ocean of your favor swells and billows,
whose treachery remains uneffaced?
When you look with the eye of mercy,
whose sins remain apparent?

O God,
Although Heaven is bright and beautiful beyond compare,
without the vision of you it is painful and searing.
Although musk is sweet-scented,
it has not the life-giving breath of your odor.
A beautiful and pleasant station is Paradise,
but it has not the splendor of your lane.

O God,
If I devote but a moment to you,
how then could I fancy houris and mansions in Paradise?

O God,
Beauty is yours alone:
All else is hideous.
Ascetics are given Heaven as a wage.

O God,
If my body is a sinner,
my heart is obedient.
If I am an evildoer,
Your clemency is my intercessor.

O God,
Would that Abdullah had turned to dust
that his name could be effaced from the register of
existence!

KHWAJA 'ABDULLAH ANSARI

Yesterday I came and accomplished nothing.
Today no market was brisk because of me.
Tomorrow I shall go, unaware of mysteries.
Had I not come, much better would it have been!

O God,
Everyone fears you,
But Abdullah fears himself,
for all that comes of you is good,
But what comes of Abdullah, bad.

O God,
If all the world be caught in a whirlwind,
let the lamp of good fortune be not extinguished.
If all the world be flooded,
let the scar of ill fortune be not washed away.
Open to us a door to your acceptance
that be not shut again.

O God,
The rich pride themselves on gold and silver,
while the poor make do with what you have allotted.

O God,
Others are intoxicated by wine:
I am intoxicated by the cupbearer.[8]
Their intoxication is epheral,
but mine abides forever.

O God,
Whether I am drunk or whether I am mad,
I am among those who reside at this threshold.
Give me knowledge of myself,
for I am a stranger to all existent things.

I am intoxicated by you.
I am free from the draught and goblet.
I am your bird. I am free of the grain and the snare.[9]
You are what I seek in the Kaaba and the idol-temple.[10]
Otherwise, I am free of both these states.

O God,
In the stream of that which you will flows water.
What remedy is there for that which you will not?

O God,
You cast pearls of purity into Adam's lap.
You smeared the dust of rebellion on Satan's brow.
These two natures you mingled together.
We humbly confess that we have done wrong.
Blame us not!
It was you who stirred up the dust of temptation!

O God,
For a long time I sought you and found myself.
Now I seek myself and find you.

You were stealthily apparent, and I unaware.
You were hidden in my breast, and I unaware.
To the exclusion of all the world I sought you openly.
You were the whole world, and I was unaware.

O God,
I am aware of my own inability.
I bear witness to my own helplessness.
All will is yours. What can I will?
I want not eternal life from you,
I want not the good things of this life,
I want not my heart's desire or my soul's repose.
What I desire of you is whatever is your pleasure.

O God,
My heart labors for your sake.
Were it otherwise, of what use is a snuffed-out lamp?

O God,
What must I do to know you?
My heart's blood pours from my eyes.
I have no key to unlock the door.

O God,
Since a dog has audience at this court
qnd a stone may look upon you,
why is Abdullah despondent?
All this is given through your beneficence;
were it not so, why speak of the dog and the stone?

O God,
I may not be among your saints,
but like the dog of the Sleepers of Ephesus,[11]
I am at your gate.

O God,
When you had the flame of separation,
why did you kindle the fire of hell?

O God,
To sin in the face of your generosity is contemptible
because your generosity is eternal
and sin is of the moment.

O God,
What grace is this that you have bestowed on your friends?
Whoever recognizes you finds them,
and whoever finds you recognizes them.

O God,
If you wish to burn Abdullah,
then it will take another hell to consume him.
If you wish to soothe him,
it will take another Heaven to give him rest.

O God,
I am annoyed by those acts of obedience
that cause me to be proud:
Happy that disobedience
that brings me to my knees.

O God,
To converse with your friends is like cool water on the soul.
To converse with other than them is torment to the soul.

O God,
The rose of Heaven is a thorn in the feet of mystics.
What cares he for Heaven who is searching for you?

O God,
If the night of separation is dark,
we still rejoice,
for the morning of union is nigh.
Nonexistence was unaware of the morning of union
where I and your love were together.
If by day I see no one in whom to confide,
what difference does it make whether the night,
when I grieve for you,
be long or short?

O God,
You called, and we were slow.
Alas! alas! what we did we did in poor judgment.

KHWAJA 'ABDULLAH ANSARI

O God,
We are wholly ignorant and wholly weak.
If you would only call,
that is what we hope for.
If you drive us away,
we shall obey your command.

O God,
You called me weak, and it is so.
Whatever comes to be on my account is thus.

O God,
You exist. I exist not.
Can that which exists not demand something
from that which exists?
Who am I to do such a thing?

O God,
Everyone is lost in you.
I am anxious for you.
When you are with me,
I am as lost as everyone else.

O God,
You are all.
We are nothing.
You are mindful.
We are heedless.
This is all that needs be said:
Be not strict with us.

O God,
You are disposed to forgive,
while I am sinful.
Place me in the end at your court.

I know I am not righteous,
but place me in the end with the righteous.

O God,
'Though I may be an offender,
I am a Muslim.
If I am a sinner,
I am regretful.
If you want to punish me,
I'll obey your command.
If you have mercy,
I deserve it.
Whether the Beloved gives us agony or pleasure,
whatever comes from the Beloved is good.
We do not think of good or evil—
our intent is His pleasure and contentment.

O God,
Since all is as you will,
what do you desire of this helpless weakling?

O God,
While you were hidden,
I was all flaw.
When you came forth from the unseen,
I emerged from fault.

O God,
I know not whose daily bread I hold in my hand.
I know not in whose hand is my daily bread.

O God,
What you sewed I put on;
what you poured into the cup I drank.
Nothing has come of that for which I myself have striven.

O God,
If you chastise me for my sins,
I'll chastise you for your clemency
because your clemency is greater than my sins!

O God,
Everyone fears what may happen tomorrow,
but Abdullah fears what happened yesterday.[12]

O God,
If the pure must beg forgiveness,
what must the impure have to do?
There where the eagle will be overturned,
contemplate how the owl will be.

O God,
You beggar is happy in what he does
because your beggar is a king in this world and the next.

O God,
If our souls pass away in melancholy over you,
it is that same melancholy that causes the soul to wax.

O God,
When there comes a trace of your love,
all other loves fade away.

O God,
Your glorious Book is a keepsake from you.
Since you are present therein,
what need is there of a memento?

O God,
Smoke does not signal fire
or dust the wind

194

so much as does the external show the internal
and the apprentice the master.

O God,
We rejoice in the grief that comes of loving you:
we flourish in the plunder of your tribulations.

O God,
There is no joy without pain from you;
there is no freedom except in bondage to you.

O God,
I tremble like a willow at the thought
that I may not be of worth.

O God,
Everybody fears the day of retribution,
but Abdullah fears the day of pre-eternity[13]
because what you decreed in the beginning
will never be changed in the end.

O God,
When near to you they give signs of you
from which you are far away;
when far from you they only imagine,
but you are closer than the soul.

O God,
What sort of intoxication has overcome your select friends
that whoever finds himself
finds you
and turns his back on all else?

O God,
What is more painful than for the beloved to be rich
and the lover poor?

KHWAJA 'ABDULLAH ANSARI

O God,
Had he not sought aid in your favor,
how could the son of Amram[14] ever have asked to see you?

O God,
You are the manifestation of religion,
and your friends are mirrors.
One can see religion in those mirrors.

O God,
I possess that mirror in which you are reflected.
Rather, I am that mirror.
You are not separate from me.

O God,
If we are judged by our words,
then I am a king over all.
If we are judged by our actions,
then I am as helpless as a mosquito and ant.

O God,
Who am I to desire you?
Being aware of my own lot, I am less than whatever I may
think
and grow worse with every breath I take.

O God,
If it is necessary for you,
Abdullah will do whatever is proper.
If it is necessary for himself,
Abdullah will do whatever is improper.

O God,
The agony of loving you is a calamity.
Calamity from the hand of the beloved is a boon,
and to complain of a boon is wrong.

O God,
I am helpless and perplexed.
Neither have I what I know
Nor know I what I have.

O God,
Being such as I am, my search for you is blasphemous.
What am I to do?
My heart is impatient to know you.

O God,
Of the period of expectation
there remains but a day.
Of the pain of separation
there remain but a sting in the heart.

O God,
You have said that you are generous.
Therein lie all our hopes.
Since you have said that you are merciful,
we are forbidden to be despondent.

O God,
Should I complain of what is?
Or of what isn't?
It is absurd to complain of what is.
It is wishful thinking to complain of what isn't.

O God,
Without the vision of you, Paradise is a prison.
To take a captive to prison is not the act of the clement.

O God,
We are so humiliated that we have dust on our heads.[15]
We are so regretful that our hearts are filled with agony.
We are so ashamed of our sins that our faces are pale.

O God,
If I have not been a friend,
I have not been an enemy either.
Although I persist in sinning,
still I confess your oneness.
No matter how much you take away from me,
I take nothing away from you.

O God,
I have bought what you offered me:
Of this world and the next
I have chosen your love.

O God,
Patience has fled from me,
my endurance has become feeble.
I have become a dormant seed:
It is restlessness that has sprouted.

O God,
You are the way-station;
Your friends are the way.
Therefore, neither does my heart ask forgiveness
nor is my tongue speechless.

O God,
All fires are cool in loving You;
all favors are agony without Your grace.

O God,
Although people think You are distant,
You are nearer than the soul—
yet You are more sublime than any token
that may be given of You.

O God,
Those who labor for wages are content with You,
but those who know You are indifferent to past and future.

O God,
The soul is drowned in the visible sea,
the body is veiled,
hearts are in ruins,
and eyes are faulty.

O God,
People run from affliction to joy.
I am afflicted with joy.
Everyone fears for himself in joy.
I am at one with You.

O God,
When the sea of Your favor billows,
how is it possible for the offenses of the disobedient
to show through?

O God,
You did shape us as You Yourself desired.

O God,
I am neither happy nor patient,
I am neither healthy nor ill,
I am neither close nor deprived.

O God,
When I came to know You,
I was cut off from people
and became raving in the eyes of the world.
I was hidden, but now I am found.

O God,
When I do not speak to you,
I become heavy-laden.
When I do speak to you,
my load is lightened.

O God,
This world is all deception:
Love of it is worse than of Satan.

O God,
You are capable of everything from nothing;
of everything, you resemble nothing
that one might say, "He is like *this*,"
or, "He is like *that*,"
for you are the Creator of *this* and *that*.
The celestial spheres are tamed
by your decree.
The neck of the Universe is held in check
by the leash of your control.
The unruly are bound by you.
The rebellious are broken by you.
Hell is your prison.
Paradise is your garden.
In the heavens is your kingdom.
On earth is your command.
You are hidden within the heart.
You are visible in the next world.
All power and majesty are yours.
At the Resurrection
the obedient are robed with your beneficence.
The patent of all who enjoy good fortune
bears your signature.
The heart seeks no remedy from the soul
for the pain inflicted by you.

The soul seeks no release from its agony in loving you.
Unless we speak out to someone
of the grief inflicted by you,
The odor of our seared passions will not disgrace us.

2

If you bring us to trial, we have no defense.
If you burn us, we have no endurance.

From a slave comes only sin and debaseness.
From a king comes bounty and mercy.

O Bestower of grace who has no need of anyone's exaltation,
O Bestower of favor whose bounty knows no end,
O Granter of ease with whom no one enjoys patronage,
O Avenger whom no one can deceive,
O Almighty against whom the unruly can mount no
resistance,
O Seer from whose affliction no wayfarer can escape,
O Generous one, except for your bounty,
your slaves must appear empty-handed.

Protect us lest we go astray.
Lead us to the way lest we wander.
We are negligent, but we are not unbelievers.
Lead us to rectitude, for we are destitute.
Gather us together, for we are scattered.

O Generous one, bestower of bounty,
O Seer who forgives sin,
O Eternal who is apart from our comprehension,
O One who is without peer in essence and attribute,
O Creator who guides those gone astray,
O Omnipotent who is worthy of godhood.
By your ever-abiding essence,

By your perfect attributes,
By your power and majesty,
By your splendor and beauty,
Give to our souls your purity.
Give to our hearts desire for you.
Give to our eyes your light.
Grant us, of your mercy, what is best.

O Lord,
Give life to our hearts through your mercy.
Give remedy to all pain through patience.
How does this humble slave know what ought to be said?
You are omniscient: Give whatever you know.

O God,
No tongue is capable of expressing thanks to you.
There is no shore to the ocean of your grace.
The mystery of your reality is not revealed to anyone.
Lead us on that road than which none is better.

O Lord, I want a sign of the straight path.
I want life from the matter of water and clay.
Since you have made me enjoy your favor,
I want a tongue with which to thank you.

O God,
Destroy the foundation of our *tawhid*,[16]
withhold water from our garden of hope,
torment us for our sins.

O God,
Cast the dust of shame on our heads;
chastise us for our own evil.

KHWAJA 'ABDULLAH ANSARI

O God,
Ahead lies danger and there is no way back.
Hold my hand, for I have no refuge save your grace.

O God,
To be and not to be are the same to me:
Bring me from the whirlpool of grief to the shore of joy.

O God,
You commanded us to look upon the poor and needy
with the same eye as we look upon the rich,
but you are too generous
to regard the disobedient in the next world
the same as you will regard the obedient.

O God,
Give us heart to lose our lives in your labor,
give us courage to do the work of the next world.
O God,
Give us possessions lest the door of greed be opened to us,
give us strength lest the sparrow of avarice become a hawk.
O God,
Give us knowledge lest we stumble along the way,
give us sight lest we fall into a pit.

O God,
Take me by the hand, for I have nothing to present to you.
Accept me, for I am unable to flee.
Open a door, for you open all doors.
Show the way, for you show all ways.
I give my hand to no helper,
for all are transitory:
only you abide forever.

O God,
Give me the next world, that I may abhor this one,
give me success in obedience that I may be firm in religion.

O God,
Give knowledge in which there be not the fire of desire,
give action in which there be not pride and hypocrisy.

O God,
Give us eyes to see your lordship,
give us heart not to choose to worship other than you.

O God,
Give us courage to place the ring of slavery to you
in our ears,
give us courage to taste the bitterness of your wisdom.

O God,
To find you is our desire,
but to comprehend you is beyond our power.

O God,
The sincerely devoted take pride in loving you,
and those who long and pine hasten toward you.
Through them you perform what others cannot do;
you fulfill their wishes, which others cannot do.

O God,
Give a cure, for from these stricken ones no cure comes,
give success, for from these languid ones no success comes.

O God,
Teach us to recognize knowledge:
Light a lamp lest we remain in darkness.

O God,
Preserve us all from the wiles of the devil.
Make us all aware of the plots of the self.

O God,
Give water to what you have sown,
make flourish what Abdullah has sown.

O God,
Show us your face
that we may look upon the face of no other,
open a door that we may knock at the door of no other.

Give me deliverance from the bonds of my self, O Lord.
Give me freedom from my evil self, O Lord.
I am a stranger: Make me to know myself.
Give me knowledge of myself, O Lord.

O God,
This is not living: It is torture;
this is no life: It is a foundation on water.
Were it not for your gaze of favor,
all that we do would be in ruins.

O God,
In this world the disobedience we do
makes your beloved Muhammad sad
and your enemy Iblis[17] happy.
If you torment us tat the Resurrection,
again your beloved will be sad and your enemy happy.
O God,
Don't give your enemy two occasions for happiness
and your beloved two occasions for sorrow.

O God,
If you would but once call me your slave,
my joy would surpass the Throne of Heaven.

O God,
If chicory is bitter, it is still from the garden;
if Abdullah is a sinner, he is still one of your friends.

My heart beats ever with desire for you;
my soul in my body breathes ever for you.
When plants grow over my dust,
let every leaf redolate with the aroma of my fidelity to you.

O God,
All want to look upon you.
Abdullah wants you to look upon him.

O God,
Do not throw down the banner that you yourself raised.
Since in the end you will pardon us all,
do not shame us from the beginning.

Your perfect kindness forgives all our faults.
The ring of slavehood to you is in all our ears.
Lift, O Lord, of your grace, the burden of sin,
from all our shoulders on the day of tribulation.

O God,
We stand as a pawn on this chessboard:
Wherever we place our rook, a knight charges us.
Since our queen of obedience goes astray,
at that hour when we shall be checkmated by death,
preserve us from the elephant-faced demon.[18]

O God,
Neither are you unjust that I should say, "Beware!"
nor do you owe me anything
that I should say, "Let me have it!"
Since you raised me up in the beginning,
put me not down in the end.
I am your guest: Keep me as you will.

O God,
Give us whatever you will.
If you do not will wheat, then give us bread!

O God,
Preserve Abdullah from three afflictions:
from the temptation of the devil,
from the desires of the flesh,
from conceit in ignorance.

O God,
You made Creation gratis.
You provided sustenance gratis.
Have mercy on us gratis:
You are God, not a merchant!

I am a disobedient slave. Where is your pleasure?
My heart is dark. Where is your light?
If you grant us Paradise in accordance with our obedience,
that is barter. Where are your favor and bounty?

O God,
If you send us to hell, we'll raise no objection.
If you send us to Paradise, unless your beauty be there,
we'll not have it.
Fulfill our desire, for all we seek is union with you.

On Doomsday lovers have no concern for Resurrection.
Lovers have no concern but to behold union
with the beloved.
If I am taken from your lane toward Paradise,
I'll not place my foot there unless I have a promise
to see you.

O God,
Grant us protection that we may dwell in the lane of your
love;
grant us a tongue with which we may render you thanks.

O God,
Bu-Jahl comes from the Kaaba,
and Abraham from the idol-temple.[19]
Everything depends upon your favor:
The rest is just pretext.

O God,
There is light in obedience,
but everything is by your favor.
We must have your mercy:
The rest is empty fable.

There where divine favor is,
iniquity is an ascetic's labor.
There where omnipotent wrath is,
the Muslim devotee is a churchman.

O God,
If I am not worthy of the trust,
on the first day you knew what I was like.
Forgive my sorrowful heart,
for humanity is torment in my religion.

With your eternal knowledge you saw me.
You saw what you were buying, in spite of my faults.
You and your knowledge.
Me and my faults.
Don't send back what you once approved.

O God,
Extinguish not this lamp ablaze;
sear not this heart aflame;
rip not this curtain sewn;
drive not away this neophyte slave.

With every breath I take I sin against you a hundredfold,
Yet out of your loving kindness you disgrace me not.
I am worse than the worst in the world:
Of your kindness you have had mercy on evil me.

O God,
If I am among your friends,
remove from me this sense of obligation.
If I am among your guests,
keep me well.
Have mercy on this sorrowful heart.
Put me not in a quandry.

O God,
By virtue of the fact that you have no need,
have mercy on one who has no defense.

O Lord,
Of your generosity, have mercy on my state.
Have mercy on my incapable heart.
Place rest and repose in my agonized breast.
Have mercy on my tear-stained eyes.

O God,
Give certainly in which there be no doubt
and knowledge that be not without illumination.

O God,
Of your grace give Abdullah wine,
that his vision be not clouded by his intellect.

O God,
We were behind a veil,
and you were screened by the unseen.
When you appeared you brought us forth from our faults.

O God,
If you raise me to the gallows, let it be,
but exile me not!
If you send me to hell, that is your pleasure,
but send me not away from you!

O God,
There is no necessity for me to fly for refuge:
Before me lies danger, with no way back.
Take my hand: I have no asylum but you.

O God,
I come to your gate as a slave—
my lips full of repentance,
my tongue asking forgiveness.
If you will, ennoble me by your generosity.
If you will, demean me,
for I am ashamed and you are the Lord.

O God,
That which I desire is not so much as a pace for you.
Since your generosity is all-pervasive,

if you would glance once my way,
then all would be done.

O God,
I have bound myself to you to the exclusion of all else.
If you would have me, I will worship you.
If you would have me not, I will worship myself.
Make me not despondent: Take my hand!

O God,
If I am raw, cook me!
If I am cooked, burn me!

O God,
Your reckoning is with those who have,
and I am a dervish.
If your accounting is with paupers,
then I come before anyone else.

O God,
What value have I to be worthy of you?
If you will, chastise me.
If you will, forgive me.
You hold the key: How should I open the door?

O God,
Whoever gets along with you is called mad.
Whoever is concerned with himself is a stranger to you.

O God,
I have a secret door to you:
I see a veil and think it a revelation.
If it is reality, keep me not in doubt.
If it is negligence, make me aware.

O God,
Sorrows are joyful with the memory of you.
Happiness is delusion without the sight of you.
Give felicity in this world,
for Resurrection is a long way off.

O God,
Since you are the bestower of mercy,
take everyone's hand.
Why question us for what we have done?
Sober or drunk, take us as we are.

O God,
What am I to do with Paradise?
What games am I to play with the houris?
Give me an eye to make a Paradise of my every glance.

O God,
When I look at you, I am proud;
when I look at me, I am lost;
when I look at my self, I melt.
Look upon us that we may discard the baggage of duality.

O God,
In our hearts plant only the seed of love for you.
For these souls destine only grace and favor.
Send down on these fields only the rain of mercy.

O God,
Smear our brows with the dust of shame,
but let us not be chastised with your affliction!

O God,
Finish what you gave a taste of.
Make perpetual this lightning you made shine.
Couple the beginning of this felicity with its end.

213

O Lord,
What I, a mere beggar, desire of you
is more than a thousand kings could wish.
Everyone has a request to make of you,
but I have come to ask you for yourself.

O God,
By the sanctity of that name which you know,
by the sanctity of those attributes which you are like,
hear our plea, for of that only you are capable.

O God,
Preserve us from four things:
disgrace on the Day of Reckoning,
inattentiveness when you speak,
deprivation when you give audience,
being veiled from the sight of you.

O Lord,
Provide me with repentance.
Provide me with obedience worthy of you.
Before I finish my labor in this world,
provide me with freedom from this world and the next.

The Song of the Dervish

O God, the *qibla*[20] of those who know is the sun of your
face.
The *mihrab*[21] of all souls is the arch of your brow.
The Masjid al-Aqsa[22] of all hearts is the sanctuary of your
lane.
Glance in our direction, for our gazes are upon you.

The world is an abode of affliction and trial,
not a place of rest and repose.
Where is there room here for joy and gladness?
To be mindful of God in every condition
is then the key to salvation.

Vexed is the seeker after this world.
Rewarded is the seeker after the next world.
Glad is the seeker after the Lord.

He who desires the world is mad.
He who desires Heaven labors under a pretext:
The goal is the Lord of the House.
Some have ambition of attaining Heaven:
Some desire the Beloved.
Happy is he whose banner reads "ALL IS HE"!

O Paradise,
I am not concerned with you: Don't be so long-winded!
O Hell,
I am not afraid of you: Don't tell me about yourself!
What is happiness?

To be concerned with loving God
and to rid oneself of love for Creation.
Do you know who the traveler on the true road is?
He is one who knows what poverty is.

To be a dervish means to be a lump of sifted earth
with a little water sprinkled on top.
It means to be something that
neither harms the soles of the feet
nor leaves a trail of dust behind.

What is poverty?
An unhypocritical exterior
and a peaceful interior.
The poor has neither name nor shame.
He knows neither peace nor war.
The poor has water in the well
and bread in the unseen realm.
He has neither a concern in his head nor gold in his pocket.

This rank is not attained by putting on a cloak and cap.
This felicity is attained by the striving of an enlightened
heart.

If one abandons the rigor of knowledge
for the delights of the black-eyed houris,
the purity of his knowledge is shattered.
If a dervish seeks anything other than God Himself
from God,
the door to His response is closed.

What a happy abode is nothingness!

If you walk on water, you are wet.
If you fly in the air, you are a fly.
Fall in love in order to be somebody!

216

Fasting to endurance is a way to save on food.
Vigil and prayer is a labor for old women.
The pilgrimage is an occasion for tourism.
To distribute bread in alms is something for philanthropists:
Fall in love:
That is doing something!

Knowledge is a shoreless ocean
in which the knower's soul is a signpost.

Hallaj[23] said, "I am God" and crowned the gallows.
Abdullah said, "God" and was crowned.
What Hallaj said I too have said.
He said it aloud.
I, silently.

He who knows three things is saved from three things:
Who knows that the Creator made no mistakes at Creation
is saved from caviling.
Who knows that He made no favoritism in allotting fortune
is saved from jealousy.
Who knows of what he is created
is saved from pride.

Look to what you do,
for that is what you are worth.
True labor means neither fasting nor prayer:
True labor means defeat and needfulness.

What grief does the humble have for his daily bread?
He who conceals his affair is given no less;
He who seeks openly is given no more.
That which God has allotted neither increases one iota
nor occurs one instant sooner.

Beginners have speech on their tongues.
The advanced have neither the power to speak
nor the means to express.

If I am silent they will say I am mad.
If I speak they will say I am a stranger to reason.

God's favor comes unexpectedly,
but only to an alert heart.

Put not your hope in people,
for you will be wounded.
Put your hope in God
that you may be delivered.

Strive to become a man and one who knows pain.

O God, what have you given one
to whom you have not given reason?
What have you not given one
to whom you have given reason?

Be intoxicated but do not cry out!
Be fulsome but do not fulminate!
Be humble and silent:
A sound jug is passed from hand to hand,
but a broken one from shoulder to shoulder.
If you want salvation, become afflicted!
Seek the remaining after annihilation.
If you have, rejoice!
If you have not, seek!

Notes

Introduction

1. 'Abd al-Rahman Jami, *Nafahat al-uns min hadarat al-quds*, ed. Mehdi Tawhidipur (Teheran: Mahmudi, 1337), p. 332.

2. Khwaja 'Abdullah's ancestor, Abu-Mansur Matt, was the son of one of the Ansari, the original inhabitants of Medina who adopted Islam when the Prophet Muhammad migrated there from Mecca in 622. The descendants of the Ansar bore the title Ansari.

3. S. de Laugier de Beaurecueil, *Khwadja 'Abdullah Ansari (396–481 H./1006–1089), Mystique Hanbalite*, Recherches de l'Institut de Lettres orientales de Beyrouth, vol. 26 (Beirut: Imprimerie Catholique, 1965), pp. 25f.

4. Jami, *Nafahat*, p. 337.

5. W. Montgomery Watt, "al-Ash'ari," *Encyclopaedia of Islam*, 2nd ed. (Leiden: E. J. Brill, 1960), I, 694f.

6. de Beaurecueil, *Khwadja 'Abdullah*, p. 106; for list of extant manuscripts of this work see ibid., p. 105, n. 2; an extract in French is given in ibid., pp. 204–221.

7. Ibid., p. 76; extract in French, pp. 198–203.

8. See ibid., p. 105, for list.

9. The technical term for this knowledge/gnosis is *ma'rifat*, and one who experiences *ma'rifat* is called *'arif*. Since the term "gnostic" in English has accumulated negative connotations, the translator has been forced to use cumbersome circumlocutions such as "one who knows" in the translation of the *Munajat*. It is the knowledge of gnosis that is meant, however, and not rational or intellectual "learned" knowledge.

10. Jami, *Nafahat*, p. 336.

11. Ibid., p. 298.

12. Ibid.

13. Edited by M. 'Abd al-Hayy Habibi (Kabul, 1341/1961); extracts in French in de Beaurecueil, pp. 259–273.

14. Ed. Habibullah Amuzegar (Teheran: Danishgah, 1348) in 2 vols.

15. Ed. S. de Laugier de Beaurecueil in *Mélanges Islamologiques* 2 (Cairo: Institut Français d'Archéologie Orientale, 1954); extracts in idem, *Khwadja 'Abdullah*, pp. 172–197.

16. Ed. and trans. S. de Laugier de Beaurecueil, *'Abdullah al-Ansari al-Harawi, Les Etapes des Itinérants vers Dieu* (Cairo: Institut Francais de l'Archéologie Orientale, 1962). A collection of twenty *ghazals* from a work known in Central Asia under this title but which is probably the *Kanz al-salikin* (see below) was published and translated into Russian by V. Zhukovsky, "Pesni kheratskago startsa," in *Vostochnyya Zametki* (St. Petersburg, 1895), pp. 79–113; these poems of dubious ascription were translated from the Russian into English by L. Bogdanov, "The Songs of the Elder of Herat," in the *Journal of the Royal Asiatic Society of Bengal, Letters*, vol. 5 (1939), pp. 205–255.

17. Trans. S. de Laugier de Beaurecueil in "Un petit traité de 'Abdullah Ansari sur les déficiences inhérentes à certaines demeures spirituelles," *Mélanges Massignon*, vol. 1 (Damascus, 1956), pp. 153–171.

18. Ed. Tahsin Yazici in *Sarkiyat Mecmuasi* (Istanbul Üniversitesi, 1956), pp. 59–88.

19. Ed. and trans. S. de Laugier de Beaurecueil, "Un opuscule de Khawja 'Abdullah Ansari concernant les bienséances des soufis," *Bulletin de l'Institut Français d'Archéologie Orientale du Caire* 59 (Paris, 1960), pp. 203–239.

20. Ed. Y. E. Berthels in *Izvestiya Akademii Nauk*, series vi, vol. 20 (Leningrad, 1920), pp. 1139–1150.

21. The *Munajat* has been printed many times: under the title *Munajat-o nasa'ih* (Berlin: Kaviani, 1924); under the title *Magalat-i dilpasand-i 'arif-i rahhani . . . Abu Isma'il Khwaja 'Abdullah Ansari* (Teheran: Chapkhana-i Islamiyya, 1358/1318); a facsimile edition of the *Munajat* written by the calligrapher Mir 'Imad al-Hasani was published by the Anjuman-i Dustdaran-i Kitab (Bibliophile Society) at Teheran (Chapkhana-i Bank-i Milli-i Iran, 1333). Trans. Sir Jogendra Singh, *The Invocations of Shaikh Abdullah Ansari*, 1st ed., The Wisdom of the East Series (London: John Murray, 1939), 3rd ed. (London, 1959); trans. A. J. Arberry in *Islamic Culture* 10, pp. 369–389; trans. Lawrence Morris and Rustam Sarfeh, *Munajat: The Intimate Prayers of Khwajih 'Abd Allah Ansari* (New York: Khaneghah and Maktab of Maleknia Naseralishah, 1975).

22. Jan Rypka, *History of Iranian Literature*, ed. Karl Jahn (Dordrecht: D. Reidel, 1968), p. 235; de Beaurecueil, *Khwadja 'Abdullah*, p. 67.

23. de Beaurecueil, *Khwadja 'Abdullah*, p. 287.

24. Wladimir Ivanow, *Tabaqat* of Ansari in the Old Language of Herat," *Journal of the Royal Asiatic Society* (1923), pp. 1–34, 337–381.

25. As suggested by Père de Beaurecueil (*Khwadja 'Abdullah*, p. 288), it may be possible to reconstruct a similarity to the original *Munajat* by retracing the steps of the original redactors and extracting sentences from his other surviving works. The *Munajat*, however, has stood more or less in its present form for so many centuries that it is, in a certain way, what it has become. This little book has been cherished by so many generations of Persians that if the totality of its contents cannot be accurately ascribed to Khwadja 'Abdullah, one can only say, *se non è vero, è ben trovato*.

26. Rypka, *History*, pp. 235, 251.

Text

1. "Lord, show me [thyself] that I may gaze upon thee" is said by Moses on Mount Sinai in Koran 7:143. God's answer is, "Thou shalt never see me!"

2. "Poverty is my pride" (*al-faqr fakhri* is a saying attributed to the Prophet. It is one of the *hadiths* favored by the Sufis, who took this "poverty" to mean total spiritual disencumberment from the world).

3. Pir-i Ansar is the poetic nom de plume often used in poems attributed to Khwaja 'Abdullah. The inclusion of the nom de plume in the last line of a poem, as here, postdates Ansari by at least two centuries; nonetheless, this intense *ghazal* is traditionally included in the *Munajat*.

4. Majnun, taken from an old Arabian story, is the lover par excellence of Persian poetry. Unable to be united with his beloved Layli, Qays of the Beni 'Amir went mad (*majnun*, hence the epithet) and wandered senseless through the desert. The Sufis saw in Majnun the ideal lover who had shed his reason and abandoned his possessions and position on behalf of his beloved.

5. To "pour dust on the head" is the Persian expression for suffering abject grief and humility. The pun here (see Introduction) involves *khaksar* ("humble," literally "like dust") and *khak* ("dust").

6. See Introduction, p. 173.

7. In the Islamic version of the temptation of Adam and Eve, the "apple" familiar from the King James Bible is a sheath of wheat or grain, which accords well with the notion here of providing sustenance, or "daily bread."

8. In Persian mystical poetry, "wine" is that which intoxicates or deprives the yearning lover of his senses and rationality. The "cupbearer" (*saqi*) is the manifestation of divine Beauty.

9. "Grain" and "snare" are often found in Persian poetry in connection with birds, which are lured into the snare by a trail of grain. Here Ansari expresses his voluntaristic love for God by saying that he has no need of "draught and goblet" to be intoxicated by divine Beauty. He is as faithful to God as a tame bird and has no need of "grain and snare" to be trapped.

10. The Kaaba in Mecca is the central cult edifice of Islam. It is in the direction of the Kaaba, also known simply as "The House," that Muslims turn in prayer. In mystical poetry the Kaaba often represents adherence to the externals of Islam, while the idol-temple (*butkhana*) represents the obverse, where the true devotee, or "idolator," goes to worship his beloved idol, divine Beauty.

11. The Sleepers of Ephesus, known to Islam as the "People of the Cave" (*ahl al-kahf*), are referred to in the Koran 18:10–27. Pursued by their infidel enemies, the righteous band of monotheists were caused by God to enter a cave, where they slept for several centuries until the ungodly had perished. The Sleepers' dog, often called Qitmir, guarded the entrance to the cave all this while. Some say that Qitmir was rewarded for his fidelity by being transformed into a human.

12. In the language of Persian mystical poetry, "tomorrow" refers to the Day of Judgment and "yesterday" to a day in pre-eternity, before Creation, when God marshaled the souls of all of as-yet uncreated mankind and asked them, "Am I not your Lord?" To this they replied, "Yes. We bear testimony to that" (Koran 7.172). On the basis of this "covenant" men are responsible for obeying God as their only Lord.

13. See note 12.

14. The son of Amram is Moses. For his request to see God, see note 1.

15. See note 5.

16. *Tawhid* is declaration of God's unity. In the technical vocabulary of Sufism, *tawhid* means to recognize that the One God is the only agent and that all existence is His. Since only He exists truly, only He has the right to utter the word of ego-consciousness, "I." When Ansari asks God to "destroy the foundation of his *tawhid*," he wants his individual consciousness to be obliterated so that he can be fulfilled by God. For a discussion of *tawhid*, see Annemarie Schimmel, *Mystical Dimensions of Islam* (Chapel Hill: Univ. of North Carolina Press, 1975), pp. 146ff.

17. Iblis is the name of the Islamic counterpart to Satan.

18. On the Persian chessboard the bishop is known as the "elephant."

19. Bu-Jahl was a bitter enemy of the Prophet Muhammad in Mecca. As a citizen of pagan Mecca, he would have gone often to the Kaaba when it

housed idols. According to legend, Abraham, the monotheist par excellence of the Islamic tradition, was the son of an idol-monger. For the significance of the Kaaba vs. the idol-temple, see note 10.

20. The *qibla* is the direction toward the Kaaba in Mecca, see note 10.

21. The *mihrab* is the arched niche in a mosque that indicates the *qibla*.

22. The Masjid al-Aqsa, which stands next to the Dome of the Rock in Jerusalem, is the second most holy spot in Islam, after the Kaaba in Mecca. It was to al-Aqsa that the Prophet was transported during his Nocturnal Journey prior to his *mi'raj*, or ascent into Heaven.

23. Hallaj, the famous martyr-mystic who, because in ecstatic union with God he claimed *ana 'l-haqq* ("I am the Divine Truth"), was put to death in Baghdad in 922.

Father Brian Kennedy, with Henderson Braxton, Paul Hampton and Perry Howell, will be busy next winter carrying wood to families who run out of fuel.

R U F U S

By Father Patrick O'Donnell

strangled one priest. He
ablin' into my shell hole
ought he was a German.
cognized him as our chap-
him un. He said, 'Let's

up" songs. Out of the same deep
well comes his compulsion to make
paintings of the lovely places God
lets him see.

Doctor bills, a hard winter, and

Albert Stone, heard a
and offered a thous
lumber to put Rufus b
ness. "It's enough to gi
over", Rufus told th
they prayed for a whi

Bibliography

BIBLIOGRAPHY

Works on 'Abdullah Ansari in Western Languages

de Beaurecueil, S. de Laugier. "L'aspiration à Dieu (*raghba*), rectification de l'espérance." In *Mélanges de l'Institut dominicain d'Etudes orientales* (Cairo) 7 (1962–1963), pp. 1–20.

————. "Autour d'un texte d'Ansārī, La problématique musulmane de l'espérance." In *Revue Thomiste* 2 (1959), pp. 339–366.

————. "Esquisse d'une biographie de Khwāja 'Abdallāh Ansārī." In *MIDEO* 4 (1957), pp. 95–140; *MIDEO* 5 (1958), pp. 47–114; *MIDEO* 6 (1959–1961), pp. 387–402.

————. *Khwādja 'Abdullāh Ansārī (396–481 H./1006–1089): Mystique Hanbalite*. Recherches de l'Institut de Lettres orientales de Beyrouth, 26. Beirut: Imprimerie Catholique, 1965.

————. "Pauvreté et vie spirituelle chez 'Abdallāh Ansārī." In *Mardis de Dar-as-Salam*, pp. 65–81. Paris: Vrin, 1953–1954.

————. "La place du prochain dans la vie spirituelle d'après 'Abdallāh Ansārī." In *MIDEO* 2 (1955), pp. 5–70.

————. "Les references bibliques de l'itineraire spirituel chez 'Abdallāh Ansārī." In *MIDEO* 1 (1954), pp. 9–38.

————. "Le retour à Dieu (*tawba*), élément essentiel de la conversion, selon 'Abdallāh Ansārī et ses commentateurs." In *MIDEO* 6 (1959–1961), pp. 55–122.

Berthels, Y. E. "Grundlinien der Entwicklungsgeschichte des sufischen Lehrgedichtes in Persien." In *Islamica* 3/1 (1927), pp. 1–31.

Ivanow, Wladimir. "*Tabaqāt* of Ansārī in the Old Language of Herat." In *Journal of the Royal Asiatic Society* (1923), pp. 1–34, 337–382.

Levy, Ruben. "A Prose Version of the Yūsuf and Zulaikhā Legend, Ascribed to Pīr-i Ansār of Harāt." In *Journal of the Royal Asiatic Society* (1929), pp. 103–106.

Ritter, Hellmut. "Philologika II." In *Der Islam* 17/3–4 (1928), p. 255.

————. "Philologika VIII/1: Ansarī Herewī—Senā'ī Gaznewī." In *Der Islam* 22/2 (1934), pp. 89–100.

226

Index to Preface, Introductions and Notes

138, 139, 142, 148; as Source, 131, 142; throne of, 149, 150; union with, 131, 134, 135, 140, 142, 145, 146, 148; Unity of, 10, 22, 37, 135, 142, 145, 176, 223; will of, 130, 133, 134, 143, 173; and world, 133, 147.

137, 149; 10: 101, 141; 14: 20, 137; 17: 20, 138; 17: 80, 148; 18: 45, 145; 20: 5, 149; 21: 18, 146; 22: 46, 137; 24: 11-20, 148; 27: 34, 145; 31: 14, 148; 53: 42, 137; 57: 3, 141, 150; 65: 7, 135; 66: 8, 149; 75: 18-19, 145.

The Real, 11, 32, 35, 37, 132, 133, 135, 136, 137, 140, 145.

Revelation, 28, 35, 42.

Rumi, xv.

Rypka, Jan, 221, 222.

Sa'di of Shiraz, 176.

-Sakhawi, 34.

Salimiyyah, 15.

Saljuks, 17, 170, 174.

Salvation, 6, 11.

Sarfeh, Rustam, 221.

Satan, 223.

Saydalani, Muhammad, 174.

Schimmel, Annemarie, 223.

Self-direction, 130.

-Shadhili, Abu 'l-Hasan, 7, 20-21, 22, 23, 30, 34.

Shadhiliyyah, 3, 7, 14, 15, 16, 19, 20, 22, 23, 25, 27, 28, 29, 30, 31, 33, 34, 36, 40, 42.

Shafi'ites, 10, 20, 25, 26, 28, 34.

-Sharnubi, 'Abd al-Majid, 39, 41.

-Sharqawi, 'abd Allah, 41.

-Shaykh al-Akbar, 15, 25.

Shi'ites, 13.

Sijzi, Abu'l-Waqt, 174.

Sin, 138.

Singh, Sir Jogendra, 221.

Shirk, 132, 133, 134.

Soul, 131, 138, 146, 147.

Spirit, 131, 136, 137, 139, 147.

-Subki, Taqi ad-Din, 28, 34, 35.

A Sufi Saint of the Twentieth Century, 42.

Sufism, cf. also Gnosis, Mysticism, Path; and asceticism, 12, 22, 33, 34, 140, 172, 173; and contemplation, 8, 11, 18, 27, 33, 39, 43, 133, 136; and devotionalism, 12, 22, 33, 140; as esoteric, 7, 10, 27, 29, 132, 133; history of, xiv, 9, 10, 11, 15, 17, 18, 21, 28, 32, 33, 41, 165; the Invocation of, 29, 137, 140, 148; and Law, 10, 20, 28, 173; orders of, 3, 7, 8, 15, 16, 21, 26, 41; spirituality of, 9, 10, 12, 14, 28, 30, 33, 34, 38, 43, 171, 172; ternaries of, 135, 136, 142.

Suhrawardiyyah, 8.

Sulami, 165, 173.

Sunnah, 6, 8, 170, 171.

Sunnite, 13, 17.

Tabaqat al-sufiyyin, 173.

Tahsin, 221.

Tagi, Abu-'Abdullah, 169.

Thomas Aquinas, 16.

'Uyun al-haqa'iq, 28.

Watt, W. Montgomery, 219.

World, 135; existence of, 141, 142; exterior, 141; nature of, 134; relativity of, 137, 142, 146.

Zarruq, Ahmad, 34, 36, 40, 41, 42.

Zhukovsky, v., 221.

Index to Texts

for, 120, 124; Omnipotence of, 49, 54, 101, 115, 122, 123, 202, 209; is One, 114, 115, 125; power of, 74, 92, 97, 113, 183, 200, 203; Praise of, 73, 78, 83, 106, 126, 183, 184; Presence of, 49, 54, 58, 59, 101, 102, 112, 128, 186; Qualities of, 79, 81, 108; Realm of, 87, 107, 109; rejoice in, 118; renouncing of, 76, 102; rights of, 106; seeks man, 112, 126; Sublimity of, 100, 106, 198; thanks to, 115, 183, 185, 203; throne of, 127, 128, 207; the True King, 80, 83, 114; unity of, 110; union with, 53, 62, 71, 79, 87, 101, 102, 107, 122, 123, 191, 199, 208, 209; is veiled, 49, 50, 88, 102, 103, 121, 212; vision of, 118; Will of, 90, 95, 122, 189, 193, 211; worship of, 212.

Gnostics, 116, 119, 128; belong only to God, 68, 72, 105, 124; expansion of, 83; intuitions of, 99; seeking of, 67; shame of, 95; signs of, 64; and symbolism, 67.

Grace, 60, 61, 63, 66, 71, 77, 97, 103, 110, 116, 118, 121, 122, 126, 183, 190, 198, 200, 204, 207, 211, 213.

Hallaj, 217.

Heart, 199; blindness of, 56; illumination of, 49, 216; lights of, 48, 61, 72, 85, 86, 94, 99, 104, 109, 125; and love of God, 183, 189, 190, 197, 203, 207, 208, 210; and meditation, 49; as mirror, 49, 93; and mysteries, 184; and progress, 61; purification of, 76; as renouncing, 58, 60; sees interior, 68.

Heaven, 187, 191, 207, 215.

Hell, 190, 191, 200, 208, 211, 215.

The Hereafter, closeness of, 69, 81; and inspiration, 75; revelation in, 76; as reward, 65, 109.

Holiness, 73.

Hope, 47, 67, 70, 85, 120, 121, 126, 127, 192, 197, 203, 218.

Humility, 106, 184, 218.

Iblis, 206.

Illumination, 49, 52, 72, 93, 101, 108, 109, 128, 211.

Initiate, 51, 109, 112.

Intellect, awareness of, 55, 61; blurred, 47, 48, 211.

Invocation, 58, 59, 91, 109, 110, 126.

Kaaba, 189, 209.

Law, 78, 114.

Light, of certitude, 81; of confrontation, 53; exterior, 72; extinguished, 48; of God, 88, 112, 124, 128, 203, 208; inner, 75, 93, 94, 123; and insight, 61, 102; of intellect, 55; and invocation, 109; need for, 49; of orientation, 53; and prayer, 76; of sages, 93; and unveiling, 86.

Litany, 64, 75.

Lord, 114, 116; attributes of, 78; bounty of, 64; help of, 52; knowledge of, 60, 205; as man's end, 57, 215; requests to, 74, 95; rights of, 67, 89; seeking of, 215.

Majnun, 182.

Man, absent from God, 51, 52, 53, 75; deeds of, 48, 51, 58, 60; nature of, 54, 73, 107, 108, 189; needs, 91; placed by God, 47, 52, 64, 65, 75, 77, 93, 188, 199; is veiled, 54, 80, 81, 87, 199, 211, 214.

Masjid al-Aqsa, 215.

Mercy, of God, 61, 87, 90, 116, 118, 121, 127, 183, 186, 187, 193, 194, 197, 203, 208, 209, 210, 213.

Miracles, 78.
Moses, 182.
Muhammad, 206.
Muslims, 193, 209.
Mysteries, 184, 188, 203.
Mystics, 191.
Obedience, 200; and ego, 87; from God, 61, 66, 70, 71, 76, 122, 209; to God, 96, 100, 109, 127, 186, 192, 193, 205, 208, 214; of heart, 187; lacking, 185, 186, 191, 199, 204, 206, 207, 208; neglected, 60, 67; and pride, 191; rewarded, 204; and veiling, 80.
Other-than-He, 102, 118.
Paradise, 96, 97, 187, 197, 200, 208, 209, 213, 215.
The Path, 109, 114, 118, 124.
Poverty, 216.
Prayer, ritual, 76, 91, 116.
Predestination, Decrees of, 47, 119, 195.
The Prophet, 57, 115, 116.
Providence, 89, 91, 103.
Real, 53, 54.
Reality, 51, 114, 203.
Resurrection, 200, 206, 209, 213.
Satan, 186, 189, 200.
Self, direction, 47, 124; knowledge, 188, 213; plots of, 206; regard, 113; satisfaction, 55.

Servants, 54, 119; acceptance of, 204; attributes of, 73, 78, 79, 92, 106, 121; God's help to, 61, 64; and inspiration, 65; and lights, 114; lowliness of, 71, 123, 127, 192, 196, 197, 202, 210; and obedience, 96; obligations of, 99; secrets of, 87; seeking of, 67; showing of, 89; sincerity of, 67, 84, 88, 94, 112, 124; worthiness of, 65, 70, 83, 110, 185, 192, 195, 209, 214, 217.
-Siddiq, Abu Bakr, 115.
Sin, 60, 71, 85, 187, 190, 192, 193, 194, 197, 198, 202, 203, 207, 210.
Soul, 213; and expansion, 68; and God, 183, 184, 207; knowledge of, 83; repose of, 189, 191; suffering of, 199, 200, 201; veiled, 86; and the voyage, 107.
Spirit, 48.
Vices, 54, 79, 120, 121.
Virtue, 58, 91, 93, 120, 121.
World, 127, 184, 194, 199, 200, 206, 213, 214; and alterities, 104; and God, 189; invisible, 53, 107; and permanence, 65, 69, 81, 112, 188; and sorrow, 52, 71, 125, 215; visible, 53.